RED GUIDE

South Cornwall

Falmouth Lizard
Truro St. Austell
Fowey Looe

Edited by Reginald J. W. Hammond

Twentieth edition

WARD LOCK LIMITED
116 Baker Street, London W1M 2BB

Plans

ISBN 0 7063 1731 9 Casebound

ISBN 0 7063 1732 7 Paperback

Printed Offset Litho in Great Britain by
Cox & Wyman Ltd,
London, Fakenham and Reading

Contents

CONTENTS

Illustrations

THE RED GUIDES

Edited by Reginald J. W. Hammond

Barmouth and District
Bournemouth, New Forest
Channel Islands
Cornwall : North
Cornwall : South
Cornwall : West
Cotswolds
Devon, South
Dorset Coast
Isle of Wight
Lake District
Llandudno, Colwyn Bay
London
Norfolk and the Broads
Peak District
Wales N. (Northn. Section)
Wales N. Southn. Section)
Wales, South
Northern Ireland

SCOTLAND

Highlands of Scotland
Northern Scotland
Western Scotland

RED TOURIST GUIDES

Complete England
Complete Scotland.
Complete Ireland
Complete Wales
Lake District (Baddeley)
Complete Devon
Complete West Country
Complete South-East Coast
Complete Yorkshire
Complete Scottish Lowlands
Complete Cotswolds and Shakespeare Country

WARD LOCK LIMITED

South Cornwall

Railway Routes—Bus and Coach Services
Camping and Caravanning—Accommodation

This Guide deals with the South Cornish coast from Plymouth Sound to Porthleven and with as much of the country inland as can conveniently be visited from Falmouth, Fowey, Looe, or any of the smaller coast resorts. The northern boundary of the area so described is approximately marked by the main road (A30) running down to Land's End by way of Bodmin and Redruth and the road from Bodmin eastward through Liskeard and Callington to Plymouth, but for the benefit of motorists and others making trips beyond that boundary, notes are included on the routes to and from places fully described in the *Red Guide to North Cornwall.* A similar remark applies to the country beyond the Lizard and dealt with in the *Red Guide to West Cornwall*, and to that beyond the Tamar, which is the province of the various *Red Guides* covering the county of Devon.

Falmouth is the only resort of any considerable size in the area described in this Guide—Fowey and Looe, though towns in name, are diminutive in size—but from Plymouth Sound to St. Michael's Mount there are innumerable coast and inland villages of a less sophisticated order, yet with an apparent elasticity of accommodation which enables them to take their place among the most popular resorts of the West.

RAILWAY ROUTES

To Looe, Fowey, and Falmouth

I. From London. Looe and Falmouth are situated at the terminals of short branch connections off the main line from London to Penzance. Passengers change at Liskeard (for

Looe) and Truro (for Falmouth). Fowey is reached by bus services connecting with Par or St. Austell on the main line.

Most visitors travel to the terminal station in Falmouth but for the convenience of those bound for the higher parts of the town there is a Halt at *Penmere*, at which all trains stop. The summer schedules come into effect in mid-June and seats may be reserved throughout the year at a charge. Seat Regulation tickets are required for certain services in summer. Apply: Seat Reservation Office, British Rail, Western Region, Paddington Station, London, W.2.

II. **From the Midlands, the North of England and Scotland** there are through trains—or through carriages—to Plymouth with connections beyond. Passengers from the North travel through Shrewsbury and Hereford or via Birmingham.

Trains from the South-east of England run via Salisbury and passengers on this route join up with the main West of England services at Exeter (St. Davids).

The numerous smaller resorts along the coast and inland are all connected with the railway by bus, St. Austell, Truro and Liskeard being important terminals east of Falmouth. As a rule details can be obtained when booking hotel or other accommodation; but any Western Region station or Western National Bus inquiry office can generally supply the desired information (*see* p. 9).

To The Lizard

The most convenient main-line stations for the Lizard are Camborne and Redruth, from which Western National bus services provide connections thence to Helston and all parts of the Lizard.

COACH SERVICES

Another popular way of reaching South Cornwall is by the long-distance luxury coaches from London and main provincial centres. The fares are usually below those charged by rail and travellers are sure of a seat. The journey, however, naturally takes longer, personal luggage is restricted and seats must be booked in advance. Time-tables and particulars of fares can be obtained from Victoria Coach Station, Buckingham Palace Road, London, S.W.1. Tel.: 730–0202, or from main coach stations in the provinces.

BUS SERVICES

On account of the large number of outlying towns and villages some distance from the railway, there is need and, indeed, good bus services. Falmouth, St. Austell, Truro and Helston are the principal starting-points in the area covered by this Guide, and by one or two changes any part of Cornwall can be reached from any other. The great majority of the services are controlled by the *Western National* company (whose local agents or the Railway will supply time-tables, etc.), but there are still some privately-owned local services connecting small towns and villages, particulars of which can generally be obtained from the village inns, post offices, etc.

Gladstone's advice on seeing London from a bus might well be adopted for those desirous of getting into touch with rural Cornwall, for the local bus is often far more than a means of transport. The driver-conductors of buses serving remote, shopless villages undertake shopping and other commissions as a matter of course: they also bring out the latest gossip and copies of newspapers and indeed play a far more important part in the rural life than they probably realize.

Camping and Caravanning

Camping grounds of all kinds are readily available, and some of them—looking over golden sands to the sea—are ideal; but motorists with heavy caravans and rather light cars should be very careful when approaching some of these combes, for the roads often descend in gradients of 1 in 5 to 6.

As a rule permission to pull in or to pitch camp is readily granted. Particulars of regular caravan sites are generally available on application to the local authority.

ACCOMMODATION

There is accommodation to suit all tastes and purses at Falmouth, Fowey, Looe or the inland towns, but *early inquiry is as imperative in these well-known centres as among the numerous little hamlets and villages boasting but an inn or two.* In addition to the hotels and boarding-houses mentioned throughout this Guide, numerous cottages and farmhouses have accommodation for visitors, and here it is even more important to engage accommodation well in advance. Comprehensive lists of all types of accommodation are readily supplied on application to the local authorities.

Licensing Hours. Where licensing hours have been given, basic times are quoted. Often during summer months extensions are made.

YOUR HELP IS REQUESTED

A GREAT part of the success of this series is due, as we gratefully acknowledge, to the enthusiastic co-operation of readers. Changes take place, both in town and country, with such rapidity that it is difficult, even for the most alert and painstaking staff, to keep pace with them all, and the correspondents who so kindly take the trouble to inform us of alterations that come under their notice in using the books render a real service not only to us but to their fellow-readers. We confidently appeal for further help of this kind.

THE EDITOR

WARD LOCK LIMITED,
116, BAKER STREET, W.1.

Motoring

There are few parts of Britain more popular with motorists than the lovely district described in this Guide, for a great proportion of it is well beyond the reach of the railway and a car has become almost essential to a holiday, unless one is a strong walker or is content to remain in one place, which would be an absurd waste of opportunity in a district so rich in beauty-spots as South Cornwall.

The road system depends upon the main east-west highway running by Liskeard, Lostwithiel, St. Austell, Truro and Helston to the Land's End. It is an ancient road, laid out in the days when deep inlets of the sea had to be skirted in the absence of fords and the then impossibility of bridging; and so it touches the head of the Looe River, the Fowey River, St. Austell Bay, the Fal and Helford River, and down each of the combes run subsidiary roads serving the towns at their lower ends. These are the main roads—all good, with smooth, though safe, surfaces, and with a widely varied beauty; but in addition there are a number of smaller lanes which climb the intervening hills in a way that can be described at times as nothing less than audacious, and which link up the large number of hamlets and villages which provide holiday quarters for so many motorists each summer.

Of the **Ferries** only three need be mentioned here: that at Torpoint, crossing the Tamar to Plymouth; that between Fowey and Bodinnick; and that across the Fal to and from St. Mawes at King Harry Passage. Each of these carries cars at a fare of about 10p. to 25p. according to size.

ROAD ROUTES TO THE WEST

Routes to the West, whether from London or from the Midlands (*see* p. 14), converge on Exeter, beyond which there is a choice of routes influenced by one's destination and one's willingness to accept rugged scenery as adequate compensation for numerous long and steep hills.

The most direct route from Exeter to Looe and the eastern part of the area included in this Guide is over Dartmoor, by Two Bridges and Yelverton, to Plymouth, where the Hamoaze is crossed by Torpoint Ferry (alternatively by the new Tamar Road Bridge, *toll*); but the road is very hilly, rising to 1,400 feet above the sea. A variation of this route leaves the Yelverton road at Two Bridges and descends to Tavistock, which can also be reached (more easily) from Okehampton, on the Land's End road. But beyond Tavistock again the road is hilly.

The easiest route to Plymouth from Exeter is *via* Ashburton; but the best road, in the long run, to all the places described in this Guide is the Land's End road (A30) *via* Okehampton and Launceston, which crosses Bodmin Moor.

A further influence in choice of road is the acute congestion of traffic in Exeter during the season. At such times it is advisable to leave the main road at the by-pass, a few miles east of the city, and to make for Ashburton by way of Countess Wear Bridge (over the river Exe) and Chudleigh. From Ashburton the road crosses Dartmoor by Two Bridges to Tavistock. Cornwall is entered at Gunnislake, high above the Tamar gorge, a few miles farther, and so on by Liskeard, Lostwithiel, etc.

The Land's End road (A30) leaves London by way of Hammersmith and the Great West Road, and continues by Staines, Basingstoke and Stockbridge to **Salisbury** (81½ miles from London). (A good alternative route is A303 which runs *via* Andover, Amesbury and Wincanton, rejoining the Salisbury route near Honiton.) From Salisbury it is 20 miles to **Shaftesbury,** whence the road is unmistakable to **Sherborne, Yeovil** (122 m.) and **Exeter** (170 m.).

During the height of the season it is wise to give the congested streets of Exeter a wide berth, but those who desire to halt and see something of Exeter should follow the main road to High Street, whence a turning on the left will lead to the Cathedral and the large car park in the Close. (The *Red Guide to Exeter* will be useful.)

Those who wish to pass through Exeter and yet avoid the

busiest part of the city should keep to the left at the fork on the outskirts, and by Magdalen Street, South Street and prominently indicated continuations reach the all-important bridge over the Exe. (For alternative routes from Exeter, *see* p. 15.) Cross the bridge at Exeter and go straight ahead along Cowick Street, which becomes the Okehampton road (turn to *right* after descending hill a mile out of Exeter). Westward of Exeter the scenery is grander and soon, to the left, there are good views of the northern heights of Dartmoor, which the Bodmin road skirts all the way to **Okehampton.** Thence to **Launceston,** an ancient town set on a hill, is a run of 19 miles. At top of hill turn to right, through gateway, in 100 yards turn to left through Market Place, and then go down to the right, keeping to the left at the cross-roads on the hill. To avoid the town, turn very sharp left at top of hill into Launceston, on to the by-pass, rejoining main road at far end of town. The way is now clear for the fine 20-mile run across the moors to **Bodmin.**

Bodmin to St. Austell, for Mevagissey and Roseland resorts. At the fork just beyond Lanivet, and 3½ miles from Bodmin, keep to left. The road runs through the China Clay district and enters St. Austell at the west end of the main street. For Mevagissey turn sharp right then left at traffic lights and left again on to by-pass; for Truro, sharp right and keep straight on; for Portscatho, St. Mawes, etc., sharp right, then left on to Tregony road 4 miles on.

For **Truro, Falmouth and the Lizard** keep to the right at Lanivet fork, some 3½ miles from Bodmin, and ascend past the Wireless Station. For some way road and railway run side by side; 2½ miles beyond St. Dennis, where they part company, is Penhale fork, where keep to the left for Ladock and **Truro.** For Falmouth and the Lizard cross the bridge on entering Truro, bear right and follow main road to the broad space known as Boscawen Street, where turn *left*. The road is now hilly, but uneventful past Perranarworthal to cross roads at top of hill, where turn sharp down to left for Penryn and **Falmouth.**

For **Helston and the Lizard** keep straight on (*see* p. 18).

From the Midlands and the North

routes converge on **Gloucester,** whence it is 34 miles by way of A38 or M5 to **Bristol** or **Avonmouth. Bristol** is entered by Whiteladies Road and Queen's Road, on the left of which are the Art Gallery and the University. Go down Park Street to College Green, bear round to left and then round to the right, across the head of the dock. Now go straight ahead, up Baldwin Street, which leads to Bristol Bridge. On the far side of the bridge is the right-hand turning (Redcliff Street) which becomes the Bridgwater road—a splendid modern highway for a great part of the 33 miles. (M5 by-passes **Bristol** city centre). From **Bridgwater** it is 11 miles to **Taunton,** and thence to **Exeter** is 31 miles.

To avoid Exeter, take the road on the right, some 15 miles from Taunton, for Tiverton, whence follow the Exeter road for about 4 miles to the road (also on the right) for Crediton and so to Okehampton. This is a hillier route than the main road, but is worth following during the season, when Exeter is acutely congested with traffic.

Thence the route is as already described. By the shortest route the distance from Gloucester to Falmouth is just under 200 miles; from Worcester about 235 miles; and from Birmingham 255 miles.

Alternative Route from Bridgwater

If time and distance are not all-important, a very fine alternative route from Bristol is to take the *Watchet* road out of *Bridgwater*. From here, follow the north Somerset and Devon coastal road through Blue Anchor, Minehead, Porlock Toll Road, Lynmouth, Ilfracombe, and thence *via* Lee, Morthoe, Woolacombe, Croyde and Saunton Sands to Barnstaple, calling at Instow, Bideford, Westward Ho! and Appledore. Continue on to Clovelly and Hartland, where turn south-east for Bude, Stratton, Crackington Haven, Boscastle, Tintagel, Camelford, Wadebridge and St. Columb Major to Fraddon, at far end of which bear left, *via* Ladock, for Tresillian, Truro and Falmouth. Fork right for Redruth.

For Fowey and Looe take the Bodmin road out of Wadebridge, whence it is some 18 miles to Fowey and about 25 miles to Looe. If coming from London, take the Basingstoke road and continue *via* Amesbury, Stonehenge, Warminster, Frome, Shepton Mallet and Glastonbury, joining the route just described at Bridgwater.

Alternative Routes from Exeter

(*For by-pass route via Countess Wear, see* p. 12.)

Routes via Tavistock. About 1½ miles beyond Exeter Bridge keep straight ahead when the Bodmin road swings to the right. Longdown Hill soon provides a foretaste of the heavy gradients on this route, though the scenery is compensation, especially beyond Moretonhampstead. At Two Bridges keep to the right, and shortly Princetown is seen on the left and the road begins the gradual decline to Tavistock.

Those for whom Dartmoor hills have no attraction can reach Tavistock more easily by following the Land's End road to Okehampton and then running down the western flank of Dartmoor to **Tavistock.** Now the road, already undulating, becomes definitely hilly.

Continuing from Tavistock, the *Tamar* is crossed at Gunnislake, and from the top of the long hill that follows there are grand views to the left of the lake-like waters around Plymouth. **Liskeard** is reached 18 miles from Tavistock, and a turning to the left leads down to **Looe.** The westward road turns to the right in the town, however, soon descending rather steeply past one of Brunel's striking railway viaducts. **Lostwithiel** is entered by a long descent from which the by-pass diverges on the right. Climb the far side of the valley, descend and climb again, and the turning for **Fowey** will be found on the left a little short of the top of this hill.

For **St. Austell,** however, keep to the main road, which soon runs steeply down to a level-crossing at the entrance to St. Blazey. Cross the line, bear left and at fork half a mile farther on bear up to right for Mount Charles. Just beyond the railway bridge a mile farther on bear to the left for the St. Austell by-pass; for the town keep straight on.

Routes via Plymouth. Cross the bridge at Exeter as already described (or take the Countess Wear by-pass as detailed on p. 12), and turn off to the left along the road which by Chudleigh, Ashburton and South Brent skirts the southern edge of Dartmoor to **Plymouth,** where bear as nearly as possible straight ahead to Devonport and the capacious ferry to **Torpoint.** The crossing is made in five minutes, and there is a fifteen minute service. From Torpoint the route is to Anthony, where keep to the right at the fork, and so to Polbathic, Trerule Foot and Liskeard. Then as above.

The new Tamar Toll Bridge now provides an alternative crossing of the Tamar.

Car Runs in Cornwall

I. THE LAND'S END

The country covered in this excursion is described in the *Red Guide to West Cornwall*

Leave Falmouth by A39. At Penryn bear right across the river and almost immediately turn left and ascend the steep hill through the town—A394 as far as Penzance. A fine, fast route, high and breezy, 600 feet above the sea at Long Downs a few miles out of Penryn. Descend the steep hill through the ancient town of **Helston** (famous for its annual Furry Dance) and on reaching the memorial gates, bear left, then right at foot of hill, passing through the cattle market, *en route* for **Marazion** (10 m.) on the shores of beautiful Mount's Bay. **St. Michael's Mount** (*National Trust*) stands out to sea and at low tide one can walk to it by the causeway (boats ply at other times). The Chapel and Terraces are open (*fee*) on Wednesdays and Fridays at 10.30 a.m. and noon, and 2 and 3.30 p.m. June to September, additional rooms Mondays (*fee*).

The visitor making only a brief halt will probably be less interested in **Penzance** as a town than as a view-point. Well placed overlooking Mount's Bay, it commands views that have been committed to canvas times without number. **Newlyn,** beloved by artists, lies a mile or so to the right as we stand looking seaward; to the left St. Michael's Mount rises from the floor of the Bay very beautifully, and beyond, the coast can be discerned as it runs seaward to form the western buttress of the Lizard promontory.

Unless it is desired to make a detour in Penzance, one keeps straight ahead along the main thoroughfare of the town. Beyond the tall pillared Market House keep to the right and then go to the left, in front of the Public Buildings, and so by Alverton Road to Alverton Bridge, beyond which, at "Mount Misery," keep to the left, and the road (A30) is then unmistakable all the way to **Land's End,** 36 miles from Falmouth.

Those with time and the desire to explore the coast more thoroughly should from Penzance follow the Promenade westward to Newlyn, where turn left. Climb to old village, with Harbour on left, and continue past the

Penlee Stone Quarries to quaint little **Mousehole** (*narrow streets*). Here turn inland if it is desired to see **Paul,** but the best approach to **Lamorna** is to keep the coast road beyond **Mousehole** and go up Reginnis Hill, thence following the signposts to Castallack and Lamorna. This road continues past the Old Mill and over the Lamorna river to the Cove. Thence one returns up the valley to the main road. As the next hill is climbed there appear on the right the two tall stones known as the **Pipers,** and a few hundred yards farther, just beyond a sharp bend of the road, the **Merry Maidens** can be seen in a field on the left. Two miles farther is Penberth Hill, with a sharp elbow and a short stretch of very steep gradient—leading to tiny **Penberth Cove**—and at the top of the following hill turn sharp up to the left for **Treen,** where the car may be left (every odd corner is labelled "Car Park") while the **Logan Rock,** down on the coast, is visited on foot.

From Treen return to the main road, bear to left and in about ½-mile a turning on left leads down to **Porthcurnow.** This is also a *cul-de-sac,* so again return to main road and turn left. At the Forge in about a mile turn left for Pendower Beach and Bosistow, but for Land's End turn sharp to right, and after negotiating further bends and taking what looks like a short cut through a farmyard, emerge on the main Land's End road a little south of Sennen.

Compared with some neighbouring scenes, the **Land's End** is apt to disappoint. "We imagine England's utmost cape to be a narrow tongue thrust out from the firm shore, along which we may walk to meet the advancing waves. But we find the reality to be merely a protruding shoulder or buttress of the vast irregular bluff that terminates the country."

Within sight of the Land's End on a clear day are the Isles of Scilly, 28 miles distant; while nearer, less than 1½ miles west from Land's End, the **Longships Lighthouse** rises to a height of 52 feet above a rock, itself 60 feet high. Seven miles off the coast to the south is the **Wolf Rock.**

About a mile inland from the hotels and parking place is Sennen Churchtown, with its "First and Last" Inn—a title no longer appropriate—and beyond the village, down a very steep decline on the left, is the hamlet of **Sennen Cove,** which can also be reached by walking along the cliffs from the Land's End.

Unless it is specially desired to do so, do not take the main road at the fork beyond Sennen, but keep to the left and return from the Land's End by way of **St. Just,** the north coast and St. Ives. The first part of the route is very winding, the scenery rather bleak and marred by ruined mines, and the villages depressing, but after **Zennor** the road runs along heather-clad hillsides, with grand sea-views.

St. Ives, just under 20 miles from the Land's End, is entered by a long and very steep descent. For Hayle and the homeward route turn to the right on reaching the main street; but for the harbour turn left, then right and left again to the quay. The charms of St. Ives centre about its Harbour, always interesting, with its gulls, its boats and—no less—its boatmen; but at every turn a quaint or picturesque building confronts one and there is every temptation to linger.

Our road leaves the town by a steep climb affording magnificent views. Beyond Carbis Bay we run smoothly down to **Lelant** (sharp turn to right) and at foot of hill turn left and in half a mile again left for **Hayle.** Pass under viaduct, keep left and again thread an arch and then follow the riverside road round to the right and so out on to the broad highway which in a few miles brings us to **Camborne.** Three miles farther is **Redruth** (do not take the by-pass), through which one descends steeply, turning to the right at the foot of the hill and so to Penryn and Falmouth. For Truro, St. Austell and places farther east keep straight ahead in Redruth or use the by-pass.

II. THE LIZARD

The road from Penryn and Falmouth joins that from Truro and places eastward on Long Downs, as mentioned in the previous tour. About a mile westward a road on the left goes off to **Gweek,** 1½ miles beyond which it crosses the Helston–St. Keverne road and comes to the main highway between Helston and Lizard Town. Turn to the left, and almost at once there is a turning on the right for **Gunwalloe Sands.** It should be noted, however, that this road does not go beyond Gunwalloe Church, a belt of sand and a stream preventing passage for cars. The best course for those who wish to see Poldhu and Mullion as well as Gunwalloe is to continue along the Lizard road to the *Wheel Inn,* and take the turning for Cury and Poldhu. After passing the Mullion golf links this road reaches the bridge at the head of **Poldhu Cove.** Cross the bridge for Mullion; but for Gunwalloe climb the hill on the north side of the Cove, the road coming out on the seaward side of the golf links. *Do not drive downhill* towards Gunwalloe, as cliff falls make the road dangerous and in any case one would land on soft sands. The car should be left at the top of the hill and Gunwalloe Church visited on foot.

Return to Poldhu, cross the bridge and ascend to **Mullion Village.** For the Cove keep straight ahead, turn right and in half a mile avoid road on left for Predannack. The route then enters the combe terminating in **Mullion Cove.**

Return to village and turn right, keeping to right again at far end of street. The main road is regained at Penhale, and on left the church of Ruan Major is soon seen peering above the trees. Two and a half miles farther south on the right is the toll road across the moors to the head of **Kynance Cove.** Avoid this turning and continue south for the straggling and somewhat ugly village known as **Lizard Town.**

There are many parking places here. At **Polpeor Cove** (reached in ¾ mile by the rough and narrow continuation of the main road) was the former Lizard Lifeboat station now removed to Kilcobben.

A whole day would be needed for a thorough investigation of all the coves and villages on the eastern side of the Lizard, but motorists should contrive if possible to see Cadgwith and Coverack, even if the more softly beautiful villages bordering Helford River have to be left unvisited.

For Cadgwith retrace the Helston road for a couple of miles from Lizard Town, and there take a sharp right-hand turning leading to Ruan Minor. Turn right in village and then sharp left. In about half a mile the narrow lane begins the long, steep and winding descent to **Cadgwith,** and motorists at all doubtful regarding brakes or gears would be well advised to leave the car at the top and walk down to the Cove.

Return to Ruan Minor, turn left at church and take *second* turn on right (the first leads to Poltesco by a very hilly lane), and after crossing the Poltesco Valley ascend to the fine road crossing Goonhilly Downs, a great breezy expanse of heather. At Traboe Cross the road we are on meets the St. Keverne–Helston highway. Turn right and in about 2½ miles a right-hand turn leads down to **Coverack** with its whitewashed cottages and miniature harbour.

By this time most motorists will find it necessary to turn

for home—the highway back to Traboe Cross (B3293), runs straight to Helston—but those with an hour to spare are recommended to explore the villages along Helford River.

From Coverack return to the main road and turn right for **St. Keverne,** whence go to **Manaccan,** a village built high on a hill. Do not ascend to Manaccan, however, but take a right-hand turning just short of it leading to **St. Anthony-in-Meneage** —a charming road among the trees overlooking the river. At St. Anthony turn up to the left beyond the church and keep round to the left; but do not overlook the backward views over Falmouth Harbour to the white lighthouse at St. Anthony in Roseland. At first cross-roads take the turn on the right and soon begin the fern-lined steep descent through woods to **Helford,** a lovely little village given up to boating. Re-ascend the hill to the cross-roads, where turn right for **Mawgan,** on a creek of the Helford River. From Mawgan it is but a mile or so of delightful road to **Gweek,** at the head of a creek of the Helford River, whence the way home retraces the outward route.

III. NEWQUAY, PERRANPORTH AND THE NORTH COAST

At the western end of Truro's wide main street turn up to the right, passing the west front of the Cathedral. In about 5 miles the Bodmin–Redruth road is reached just short of Zelah, and by turning right a road on the left will be found which in about 7 miles leads to Newquay.

From St. Austell turn up at the western end of the narrowest part of the main street. The road ("To Bodmin") leads through the China Clay district. Three miles from St. Austell, and just beyond a railway bridge, turn off to the left, passing the **Roche Rocks** and crossing the main highway near Roche station. Just beyond this turning another road goes off to the left and leads by St. Columb Major to Newquay.

Newquay is the largest resort on the north Cornish coast. It has fine cliff scenery, magnificent sands, dry and bracing air of remarkably equable temperature. Towan Head, a fine natural pier covered with springy turf, runs nearly a mile out to sea, and on each side of the headland is a fine bay. The town and its environs are fully described, with town plans and illustrations, in the *Red Guide to North Cornwall* in this series.

Leave Newquay by Trenance—the route by which it was approached—and, bearing right over Trevemper Bridge in 4 miles, at far end of Goonhavern, turn right for **Perranporth.** As a seaside resort Perranporth is young, but it is making rapid progress and is obviously destined to become a flourishing town. (Car park overlooking sands.) It lies in a fairly large valley, opening on to a fine two or more miles expanse of clean sand at low water—a delightful playground for children. Among the cliffs are fine archways and rock passages.

Perranporth and its surroundings are fully described in the *Red Guide to North Cornwall.* Here mention may be made of the fine walk northward along the sands and over the dunes to the "Lost Church of St. Piran"—the carefully sheltered remains of what is claimed to be the earliest Christian building in England.

Three miles south of Perranporth as the crow flies and 4½ miles by road is **St. Agnes,** its Beacon (630 ft.) a landmark for miles around, and its beautiful **Trevaunance Cove** an ever-popular little resort, enclosed by towering, rocky headlands.

Leave St. Agnes by Beacon Drive, which affords magnificent views both up and down the coast, and shortly turn right for **Porthtowan** and **Portreath.** The latter is approached by a deep combe, with steep hills on either hand. The strip of sand is the playground for many youthful residents of Redruth, Camborne, Carn Brea, and the neighbourhood around.

Leaving Portreath by the steep hill on the west side of the valley, turn to the right at the top, soon passing *Tehidy*, now a sanatorium—the Cornwall County War Memorial. In the days when Tehidy was the home of the Basset family a Mineral Tramway ran from here to the harbour. The steep incline will be noticed as one rounds the harbour property, together with the old rails which cross the road at this point.

Beyond Tehidy the road skirts the North Cliffs to Gwithian; the motorists who halt at the top of Deadman's Cove and Hell's Mouth to look down into the fine rocky coves just off the road, and along the coast northwards past St. Agnes Beacon to Trevose Head, will find it worth while.

On nearing **Gwithian** we have a magnificent view of beautiful St. Ives Bay. On reaching the main route at Hayle, turn left, and return home by Camborne and Redruth as in the Land's End tour.

IV. BEDRUTHAN STEPS AND NEWQUAY

(See the *Red Guide to North Cornwall.*)

From Truro take the St. Columb road, A39, *via* **Tresillian, Ladock** and **Brighton,** joining A30 short of Fraddon, where fork left for St. Columb Major. A mile short of that lofty village the road from St. Austell (mentioned in previous excursion) comes in on right, and here turn left (i.e. westward) and follow the Vale of Mawgan past pretty St. Mawgan village (with some notable stone crosses) to **Mawgan Porth,** a sandy bay on the coast which is fast developing into a resort. Here turn right up the hill, and the **Bedruthan Steps** tea-house and car park will soon appear on the left.

The cliffs are high and precipitous, and carpeted with soft turf and luxuriant heather, and from the sandy beach below rise huge old grey rocks of queer shapes and contortions, capped with green turf and with the vivid blue-green sea creaming round their bases. Legend says that the huge detached masses known as Bedruthan Steps were stepping-stones for the giant Bedruthan—hence the name. There are numerous caverns: great chambers and halls carved out by the sea. At new and full moon low water is at 12 noon (Greenwich—not "summer"-time). It is regrettable that due to cliff falls there is now no public access to the sands, and one has to be content with the view from the clifftop.

From Bedruthan one may continue to follow the coast to **Watergate Bay** and **Newquay:** or by turning to the left (i.e. northward) on leaving the vicinity of the Steps, **Padstow** can be visited and the return made by St. Columb Major. Between Bedruthan and Padstow are many attractive sandy coves.

V. ST. MAWES, PORTHSCATHO, ST. JUST-IN-ROSELAND

Motorists who would like to explore the beautiful Roseland peninsula should take the Truro route from Falmouth (A39), a fine undulating road with distant views from the high ground. In roughly 9 miles turn right for *King Harry Passage* at side of Playing Place Garage, passing through the hamlet of Penelewey (*Punch Bowl* and *Ladle Inn*) and 2½ miles on, the river Fal is crossed by the Steam Chain Ferry (cars 20p. single journey). The river, flanked by wooded hills, is over an eighth of a mile wide at this point and the scenery beautiful in the extreme. On reaching the other side, proceed up the steep and winding tree-lined hill and take first turn on right on reaching the top (B3289). St. Just Lane is entered in 3 miles. Here the first turn right leads steeply down the narrow, thickly-wooded lane to *St. Just-in-Roseland* Church. *St. Just Pool* lies a quarter of a mile beyond. Retrace the route up to St. Just Lane where turn right (A3078) for St. Mawes, and on topping the rise there are extensive views over and beyond Falmouth Harbour. In three-quarters of a mile stop at the narrow lane on right (which leads back to St. Just Church), and walk a few yards to the bend. A magnificent panorama is unfolded. Continuing, bear right on reaching garage, after passing a water tower. Here proceed with caution as shortly the road drops steeply round St. Mawes Castle, with an acute left-hand bend, to enter *St. Mawes*. Follow the shore road right round the residential portion of the town (view up Percuil River) and rejoin the St. Just Lane route by the garage, where go ahead (A3078) turn right at St. Just Lane then in just over 1½ miles turn sharply back to right for **Gerrans** and **Porthscatho.** Leave Porthscatho by coast road (sharp turn right up hill) and in 2½ miles turn right for **Pendower Beach.** This is a *cul-de-sac*, but there is a miniature car park which allows room to turn and retrace the route to the main St. Mawes road, where turn right, ascend the hill and at top turn left. After passing through the hamlet of **Treworthal** (narrow lanes), turn sharp left for **Philleigh** (*Roseland Inn*). The route is now unmistakable to King Harry Passage and the Ferry, and, in roughly 12 miles, Falmouth is regained.

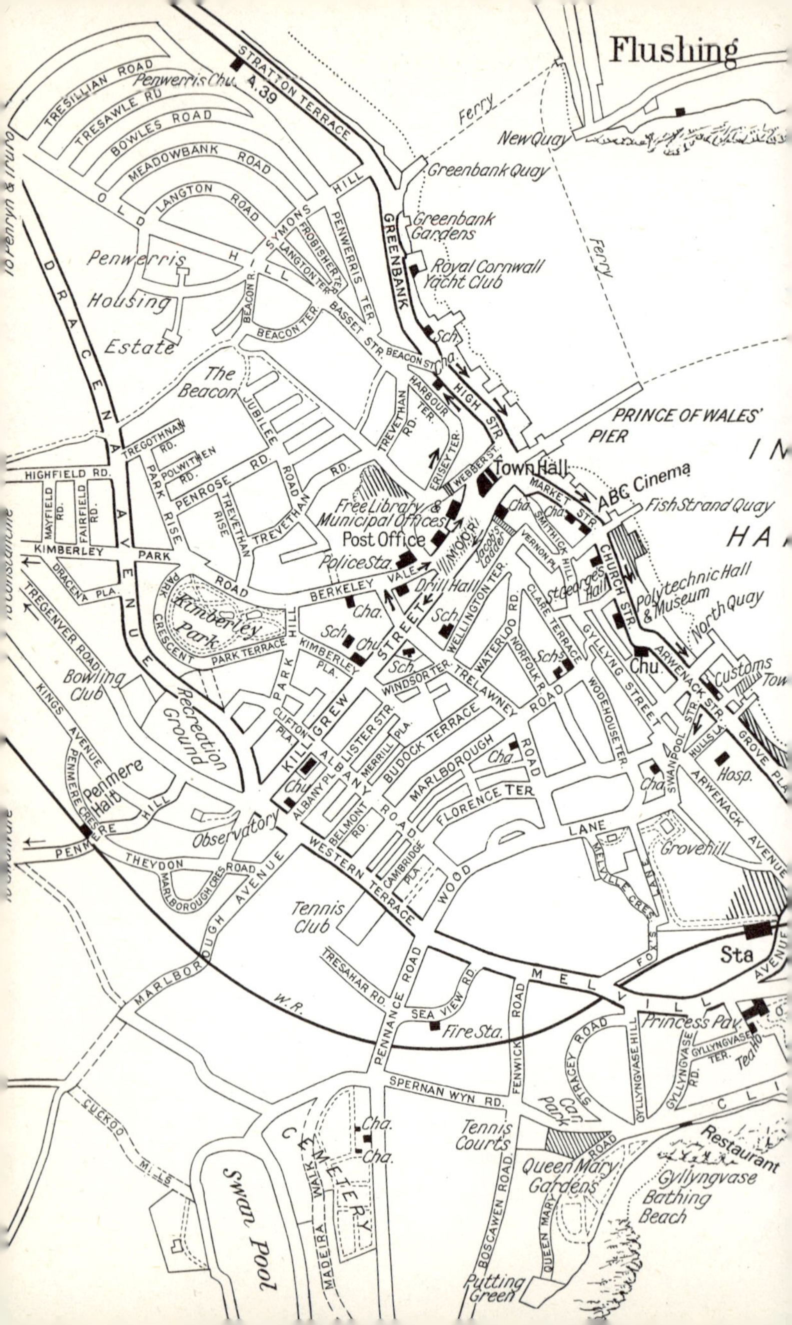
Flushing
New Quay
Ferry
Ferry
Greenbank Quay
Greenbank Gardens
Royal Cornwall Yacht Club
STRATTON TERRACE
A.39
Penwerris Chu.
TRESILLIAN ROAD
TRESAWLE RD
BOWLES ROAD
MEADOWBANK ROAD
OLD LANGTON ROAD
SYMONS HILL
PENWERRIS HILL
FROBISHER TER.
LANGTON TER.
PENWERRIS TER.
GREENBANK
Penwerris Housing Estate
BEACON R.
BEACON TER.
BASSET STR.
BEACON ST.
Sch.
Cha.
HIGH STR.
HARBOUR TER.
The Beacon
JUBILEE ROAD
TREVETHAN RD.
PRINCE OF WALES' PIER
DRACENA AVENUE
TREGOTHNAN RD.
POLWITHEN RD.
PENROSE RD.
TREVETHAN RD.
ERISEY TER.
WEBBER ST.
Town Hall
MARKET STR.
ABC Cinema
Fish Strand Quay
HIGHFIELD RD.
MAYFIELD RD.
FAIRFIELD RD.
PARK RISE
TREVETHAN RISE
TREVETHAN
Free Library & Municipal Offices
Post Office
Police Sta.
MOOR
Jacob's Ladder
Cha.
SMITHICK HILL
VERNON PL.
CHURCH STR.
KIMBERLEY PARK ROAD
DRACENA PLA.
VALE
Drill Hall
St George's Hall
Polytechnic Hall & Museum
North Quay
To Constantine
To Penryn & Truro
TREGENVER ROAD
PARK CRESCENT
Kimberley Park
PARK TERRACE
BERKELEY HILL
Cha.
Sch.
Chu.
KIMBERLEY PLA.
STREET
Sch.
WELLINGTON TER.
WATERLOO RD.
CLARE TERRACE
NORFOLK R.
Schs.
GYLLYNG STREET
Chu.
ARWENACK STR.
Customs
Tow
Bowling Club
KINGS AVENUE
Recreation Ground
PARK HILL
CLIFTON PLA.
KILLIGREW
WINDSOR TER.
LISTER STR.
TRELAWNEY ROAD
WODEHOUSE TER.
SWANPOOL STR.
HULLS LA.
GROVE PLA.
Hosp.
PENMERE CRES.
Penmere Halt
HILL
ALBANY PL.
ALBANY ROAD
MERRILL PLA.
BUDOCK TERRACE
MARLBOROUGH ROAD
Cha.
SWANPOOL
Cha.
ARWENACK AVENUE
Observatory
Chu.
BELMONT RD.
FLORENCE TER
LANE
MELVILLE CRES.
LANE
Grovehill
PENMERE
THEYDON ROAD
MARLBOROUGH CRES.
WESTERN TERRACE
CAMBRIDGE PLA.
WOOD LANE
MARLBOROUGH AVENUE
Tennis Club
FOX'S
Sta
AVENUE
TRESAHAR RD.
PENNANCE ROAD
SEA VIEW RD.
MELVILLE
W.R.
Fire Sta.
FENWICK ROAD
STRACEY ROAD
GYLLYNGVASE HILL
Princess Pav.
GYLLYNGVASE RD.
GYLLYNGVASE TER.
Tea Ho.
CLI
SPERNAN WYN RD.
Car Park
CUCKOO MILLS
CEMETERY
Cha.
Cha.
Tennis Courts
Restaurant
Queen Mary Gardens
ROAD
Gyllyngvase Bathing Beach
Swan Pool
MADEIRA WALK
BOSCAWEN ROAD
QUEEN MARY
Putting Green
HA
IN

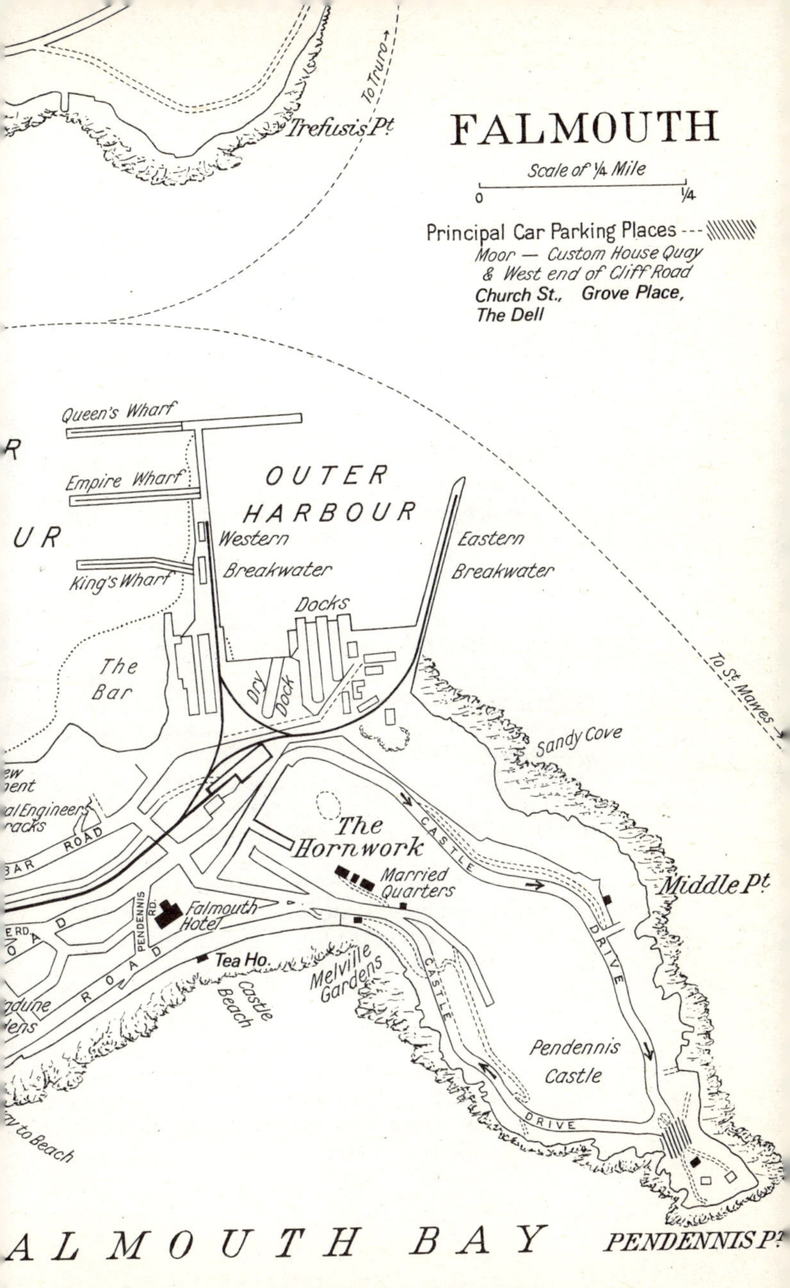
FALMOUTH
Scale of ¼ Mile
0
¼
Principal Car Parking Places
Moor — Custom House Quay
& West end of Cliff Road
Church St., Grove Place,
The Dell
Trefusis Pt
To Truro
To St Mawes
Queen's Wharf
Empire Wharf
King's Wharf
OUTER
HARBOUR
Western
Breakwater
Eastern
Breakwater
Docks
Dry
Dock
The
Bar
Sandy Cove
The
Hornwork
Married
Quarters
CASTLE
DRIVE
Middle Pt
Falmouth
Hotel
PENDENNIS
RD.
BAR
ROAD
ROAD
Tea Ho.
Castle
Beach
Melville
Gardens
Pendennis
Castle
PENDENNIS Pt
ALMOUTH BAY

Falmouth

A Town with two "Fronts"—Climate—The Story of Falmouth —The Killigrews—Charles II and Falmouth—The Packets

Falmouth has two fronts, one on the river, the other on the sea. The former extends from Penryn bridge to Pendennis Point and includes the narrow road through the main shopping centre, running from the Prince of Wales Pier to the Custom House; which, beginning as Market Street, later becomes Church Street and finally Arwenack Street. (*See* Town Plan.) This busy thoroughfare (one-way traffic) backs on to the river and here and there, from the small quays, slips and "opes" leading down to the water, glimpses of the busy harbour and docks can be obtained. From the Prince of Wales Pier and from Town and Customs Quays, there are grand views across to Flushing and extending round Trefusis Point across the Carrick Roads to the Roseland peninsula on the other side of the extensive harbour. In between there is all the life, colour and movement of a great port; ships of all types and sizes and of many nationalities, the smell of tarred rope, the scream of seagulls.

This is the oldest part of Falmouth. It faces north-east, and straggles along the western bank of the Penryn River and not the river Fal, as is commonly supposed.

The more modern portion of the town, forming the sea-front, lies just across the neck of the Pendennis peninsula. The aspect here is in complete contrast to the river front. This is Falmouth the holiday resort; here is the seashore with its grand bathing beaches, gardens and pleasure grounds; here are seats and shelters which all the year round are more generously bathed in sunshine, than, probably, any others in Britain. From the left, or eastern side of the bay, rises the majestic wooded height of Pendennis, crowned by its compact and small castle. In the centre the gently-sloping sands of Castle Beach merge into a fascinating area of rock pools teeming with aquatic life, before reaching the popular sandy bathing beach of Gyllyngvase with its beach chalets, deck-chairs, café and shops, car park, and gardens. Round the next point is the smaller Swanpool Beach, backed by lofty Pennance Point and, farther round, Maenporth beach and the estuary of the Helford River. Beyond is the eastern coast of the Lizard, with the dreaded Manacles sharply silhouetted in the distance.

As regards the Haven itself, disregarding the many small streams, no less than six rivers flow into this great anchorage. They are: Penryn River, on which the old town stands, Truro River, Tresillian River, Percuil River, Carnon River (Restronguet Creek) and last, but most lovely of all, the river Fal. *The source of the river* which gives its name to the town is at Hensbarrow Downs, Goss Moor—2 miles west of Roche, 3 miles south of Castle-an-Dinas and 7 miles west of Lostwithiel. There are innumerable picturesque creeks all round the great harbour and, before leaving for home, visitors are strongly recommended to make the trip to Truro by motor boat. In addition, a motor tour of the Roseland district should be included if at all possible. A suggested itinerary is given on p. 23 in the Motoring Section under the heading: "V. ST. MAWES, PORTHSCATHO, ST. JUST-IN-ROSELAND."

Undoubtedly one of the finest winter resorts in the British Isles, Falmouth is also pre-eminently a summer holiday haunt; and the numbers of visitors during spring and autumn testify to the fact that Falmouth is a hardy evergreen. There is no mystery connected with this perennial popularity. The simple reason is that Falmouth's climate is generally such as to render enjoyable a visit at any period of the year. During the winter there are frequently hot sunny days, with brilliant blue, cloudless skies. So glorious, indeed, are these borrowed summer days, and so perfect is the illusion, that the calendar and not the weather seems to be out of its reckoning. In summer, as can be well imagined, the local gardens present a feast of floral beauty.

Old Falmouth was not too happily placed on the side of a steep hill but the architects of modern Falmouth have built

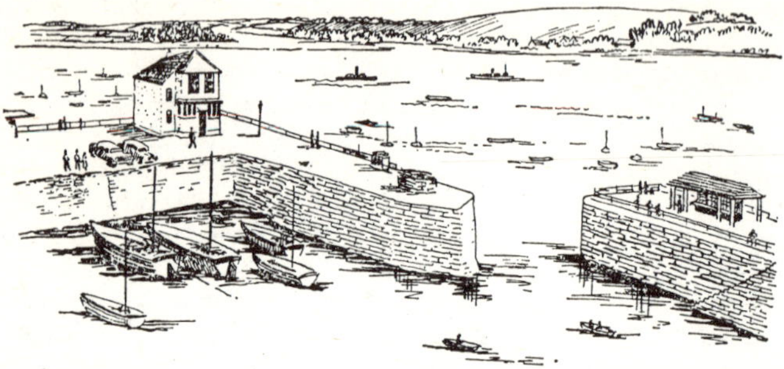

a town of which they may well be proud. The pleasant tree-shaded roads lead down to a fine promenade which, with the continuing Castle Drive around Pendennis, is a most attractive feature of this popular seaside resort.

A Note on the Climate

One of the reasons why the air of Falmouth is so beneficial to sufferers from chest and respiratory complaints is that the town enjoys an extraordinarily *equable* climate. Extremes of temperature, either hot or cold, are almost unknown. When the rest of the country is enduring heat-waves it is from 10 to 15 degrees cooler at Falmouth. Likewise, while other parts of Britain are shivering in severe cold, Falmouth is, normally, 10 to 15 degrees warmer.

The average number of hours of bright sunlight per year at Falmouth is 1,725, as compared with 1,466 at Greenwich, 1,545 at Llandudno, and 1,503 at Weston-super-Mare, recorded over a period of thirty-five years.

While the average number of days with over nine hours of bright sunshine is 44·4 in the case of Kew, at Falmouth it is no less than 64—higher than anywhere else in the country. In passing, it should also be mentioned that, unlike the French Riviera, there is very little difference in temperature between night and day in this very favoured corner of the Duchy. To sum up, the great superiority of the climate of Falmouth, and the point on which it is impossible to lay too much emphasis, lies in the *evenness* of its temperature.

The Story of Falmouth

As compared with some other towns in the Duchy, Falmouth is not of great antiquity. In Queen Elizabeth's time the only house of importance was Arwenack Manor, home of the Killigrews. In those days, the district was known as "Smithicke" and adjoined the hamlet of "Pen-y-cum-Cuic," meaning "head of the creek."

One day Falmouth will doubtless express its sense of indebtedness by erecting a statue of Sir Walter Raleigh, for it was he who first drew attention to the possibilities of the Fal estuary as a deep-water harbour on a large scale. It goes without saying that such a magnificent natural haven had long been used by local fishing and coasting vessels, and its strategic importance had induced Henry VIII to protect its entry against the French by building the castles of Pendennis and St. Mawes. Truro (11 miles up the Fal) and Tregony (now an inland town) had for several centuries carried on maritime commerce. When Sir Walter Raleigh, returning from the coast of Guinea, put into Falmouth it is not surprising that the utility of so grand a sheet of water should immediately attract the attention of such an experienced navigator. On returning to London he made representations to the Council, with a view to the establishment of a port and community to assist vessels which might need harbourage, stores, etc., and the services of an agent. There is, however, an earlier mention of the haven in history, apart from the doubtful connection of the Black Rock (midway between Pendennis and St. Mawes) with the trading for tin by the Phœnicians. In the reign of Henry IV, Jane, Duchess of Burgundy, landed here on her arrival from France as a royal bride. A glance at the "Chart of Falmouth Haven," prepared for Henry VIII and now in the British Museum, reveals only one house on the site of Falmouth, while Penryn appears as a prosperous town.

Beginnings of the Port

Early in the sixteen hundreds, arising out of Raleigh's representations, Killigrew fostered development operations. At once, these were hotly opposed by the Ports of Truro and Penryn. Their objections were, however, overruled, some say by Sir Nicholas Hals, Governor of Pendennis Castle, others say by King James, and a new settlement, combining the two hamlets mentioned above, and named Falmouth, began rapidly to take shape. From the Commonwealth Sir Peter Killigrew obtained several advantages for the new town. The Custom House was removed from Penryn to Falmouth, a market was established in 1653, a Charter granted in 1661 by Charles II and, in 1664, Falmouth, having grown rapidly, became a parish. In 1670 Sir Peter Killigrew constructed a quay and from then on maritime business greatly increased. Steady progress continued during the next twenty years as the amenities of the

port became better known, but the town owed its early prosperity to its being selected as a Mail Packet Station in 1688. The service developed and prospered over the years until, in 1827, there were no fewer than thirty-nine vessels engaged in carrying sea-borne mail from Falmouth to America, Canada, the West Indies, Brazil, Buenos Aires, Lisbon and the Mediterranean ports. As steamships began to replace sailing ships, the service from Falmouth gradually declined and was eventually transferred to Southampton in 1852. This loss of status and business hit Falmouth hard, but steam transport, plus rail service on land was obviously quicker and more satisfactory than transit by sailing vessel to a port connected with business centres only by horse-drawn coaches. When, in 1863, the railway at last placed Falmouth in direct touch with London and other big towns, the mail contracts had become too firmly established at other ports to revert to their former connections. In The Moor is a granite obelisk commemorating the gallant officers and men of H.M. Post Office Packet Service.

The Decline of the Port

It had seemed as if the commerce of the port was progressing along lines which would be permanent. Imports and exports were varied in nature and considerable in bulk. Vessels of all nations made Falmouth their destination and port of call. But from various causes the trade declined at the beginning of the nineteenth century. The introduction of steamships, while of enormous advantage to most ports, did great harm to Falmouth. The establishment of a Lloyd's signal station at the Lizard, which extends so far south into the English Channel, obviated the necessity for many large vessels to put into Falmouth for orders. The foundation stone of the now extensive Docks was laid in 1860, and three years later the Great Western Railway reached Falmouth. From the docks and the railway the town looked for great results. By using Falmouth, liners can place their passengers in touch with the railway at a point some 200 miles west of Southampton; many big liners and merchant ships come to Falmouth for overhaul and repair, and there are also facilities for coaling and oiling; but various factors beyond the control of Falmouth have combined to postpone fulfilment of those sanguine expectations—factors reflected also in the enormous tonnage of shipping which, during the slump between the two World Wars, lay idle in the Fal and neighbouring estuaries.

The natural advantages of the Fal are apparent to the merest landlubber, and several ambitious schemes have aimed at transforming St. Just, on the eastern side of the Harbour, into an ocean port. Even a hundred years ago attention was called to the conjunction at St. Just of 14 fathoms of water with harbourage sufficient for the whole of the Royal Navy of that day. In 1919 Parliamentary powers were obtained and other preparations made for the construction of a railway from St. Just to Grampound Road and the formation of dry and other docks, warehouses, etc. Financial difficulties arose, however, and the scheme lapsed.

As though in obedience to natural laws of compensation, the decline of the port occurred at a time when the construction of railways had given a tremendous impetus to holiday travel. The scenery, the climate and the fascination of the Harbour quickly called attention to Falmouth's potentialities as a resort, and public interest was further focused on the place by visits of Queen Victoria and the Prince Consort in 1843 and 1846. Warily, and with the minimum of damage to the natural beauty of the place, the Corporation did their part—the Castle Drive around Pendennis Headland was built in 1865; the same year saw the erection of the Falmouth Hotel, roads were laid out, and, as opportunity served, various choice gardens have been bought for the public use.

The fact remains, however, that the most striking characteristic of Falmouth is the contrast between the bustling port on the north side of the promontory and the serene sea views from the southern slopes. To pass from one side of the ridge to the other—a distance of only a few hundred yards—is to experience such a change of scenery as in other places can only be obtained by a journey of miles.

Gyllyngvase Beach, Falmouth

Castle Beach, Falmouth

St. Mawes

Pendower Beach, Gerrans Bay

Falmouth Town

General Information

Banks.—*Barclays, Lloyds, National Westminster, Midland, Trustee Savings Bank.*

Bathing.—*Gyllyngvase Beach*, at the western end of cliff road. With the adjoining Queen Mary Gardens this is the most popular spot on this side of the town. There are numerous beach chalets, a beach café and several shops. The sands slope gently.

At the Pendennis end of Cliff Road is the *Castle Beach*, and there are also highly popular beaches at Swanpool (*see* plan) and at Maenporth (*see* p. 47.)

Billiards.—Central Billiards Hall, Market Street.

Bowls.—A full-size green at the Recreation Ground, Dracena Avenue. Visitors are cordially welcomed by the Falmouth Bowling Club.

Buses.—Frequent services to all parts from bus terminus in The Moor. (And *see* p. 9.)

Car Parks.—The Moor; Grove Place; Gyllyngvase Beach; Swanpool Beach; Windsor Quarry; Town Quarry; Custom House Quay; The Dell; Church Street.

Churches and Chapels, with hours of service on Sundays:

King Charles the Martyr (*Parish Church*)—H.C. 8 a.m., also 1st Sunday at noon; Matins, 11; Evensong, 6.30.

All Saints' Church, Killigrew Road—Low Mass, 8 a.m.; Sung Mass, 11 (except first Sunday at 9.30); Evensong, 6.30.

Penwerris Church, Stratton Place—H.C. 9.30 and Evensong, 6.30.

Church of Holy Spirit, Mission Church—H.C. 8.30 except first Sunday at 11.

St. Mary's Roman Catholic, Killigrew Road—9.30, 11 and 6.30.

Baptist, Western Terrace; *United Reformed*, Berkeley Vale; *Methodist*, Killigrew Street and Pike's Hill—all at 11 and 6.30.

Friends, Gylling Street—11 a.m.

Plymouth Brethren.

Christian Science, 11.15 and 6.30.

Clubs.—The *Falmouth Club*, in Western Terrace, with tennis and squash courts. Other Clubs are: *Athenæum*, "Penvale," Kimberley Place; *Royal Cornwall Yacht Club*, Green Bank; *Falmouth Working Men's Club*, Bell's Court, Market Street; *British Legion*, Arwenack Street.

Coaches.—Services to Land's End, the Lizard and other famous beauty-spots.

Cricket on the Trescobeas Ground. Annual *Cricket Week*, mid-August.

Distances by Road:

	Miles		*Miles*		*Miles*
Castle Drive circuit	1½	Lizard *via* Helford	20	Penjerrick . .	4
Constantine .	7	Lizard *via* Penryn and Helston .	22	Penryn Station .	3
Helford Passage .	6	Maenporth . .	3	Penzance . .	26
Helston . .	13	Mawnan Smith .	4	Redruth . .	11
Land's End . .	36	Newquay . .	26	St. Ives . .	25
Lizard *via* Gweek	19			Truro . . .	11

Distances by Water from Prince of Wales Pier:

	Miles		*Miles*		*Miles*
Coverack . .	11	Looe . .	32	Penryn . .	1¼
Fowey . .	23	Malpas . .	7¾	St. Mawes . .	2¼
Helford . .	5¾	Mylor Pier .	2½	Truro . . .	9¼
Lizard . .	20				

Early Closing.—Wednesday, but most shops remain open during season.

Entertainments.—Band performances in Gyllyngdune Gardens; ABC cinema; variety shows, concerts and entertainment at the Princess Pavilion. Dramatic performances at Falmouth Arts Theatre.

Ferries.—Falmouth (Prince of Wales Pier)—Flushing; covered motor-ferry, every half-hour, on the hour and half-hour, from 8 a.m. to 8 p.m. (except at 1.30 p.m.).

Falmouth—St. Mawes (from Prince of Wales Pier)—At intervals daily. Also from Custom House Quay about six times daily.

King Harry—Philleigh; about every 30 minutes.

There is also a separate service to and from St. Mawes and Percuil (for Porthscatho) and St. Anthony.

Fishing.—Sea fishing in abundance at all times of the year, but June to end of September are the best months. Pollack, mackerel, whiting and chad are then the principal catches, and bass and conger eel are taken in the Helford Estuary. Good fishing grounds range from Gerrans Bay to the Manacle Rocks; also the Black Rock and St. Anthony. Mackerel may be caught by trailing several lines from a motor boat. It hardly deserves to be rated as a sport, but when the boat passes over a shoal every hook will generally have its fish and all hands work hard to free the hooks and throw them back before the shoal is lost.

Shark fishing has become popular and several boats suitable for this sport are available at Falmouth. Equipment is provided. There is a local club open to visitors.

Good fresh-water sport may be had at the Corporation Waterworks' Reservoirs near Falmouth, where fine trout are caught. Tickets, daily or longer, from Falmouth Water Engineer, Town Hall.

Golf.—An 18-hole course at Pennance, about a mile south of the town and overlooking Swanpool and the Bay. Also a 9-hole course at Budock Vean near Mawnan. Putting Green near Gyllyngvase Beach.

Heights:

	Feet		*Feet*		*Feet*
Beacon Hill .	230	Enys Hill . .	307	Roscrow Hill .	578
Budock . .	280	Observatory .	167	St. Anthony .	240
Carclew . .	266	Pendennis . .	198	Trefusis . .	210

Hotels.—*Falmouth*, Cliff Road; *Green Bank*, Harbour; *Bay*, Seafront; *Royal Duchy*, Cliff Road; *Palm Court*, Melvill Road; *Gyllyngdune*, Seafront; *St. Michaels: Melville*, Sea View Road; *Madeira*, Cliff Road; *Cheriton*, Stracey Road; *Carthion*, Cliff Road; *Rosslyn*, Kimberley Park Road; *Southcliffe*, Cliff Road; *Gwendra*, Seafront; *Pons-a-Verran*, Port Navas; *King's*, Harbour; *Morvah*, Melvill Road; *Suncourt*, Seafront; *Maenheere*, Harbour; *Membly Hall*, Seafront; and many others. Full lists from Resort Manager, Gyllyngvase Beach.

Information Bureau.—Municipal Offices, The Moor.

Library.—Public Library, with excellent reference and reading departments, The Moor. Open as stated on p. 39.

Licensing Hours.—10–2.30 and 6–10.30 Sundays, 12–2 and 7–10.30.

Newspapers.—*The Western Morning News* (daily), *The West Briton and Royal Cornwall Gazette* and *The Falmouth Packet* (weekly).

Population.—Resident, 17,550.

Post Office.—Head Office in The Moor, adjoining the Public Library. Open weekdays, 8.30 a.m.–5.30 p.m.; Sundays, 9–10.30 a.m.; Bank Holidays, 9 a.m.–noon. Sub-offices at Arwenack Street, Killigrew Road, Marlborough Road, Draceena Avenue, Pennance Road and Old Hill.

Railway.—Western Region, Platform at Avenue Road.

River Fal Trips.—Fast motor passenger-boats make frequent trips daily across the Harbour and up the Fal and Truro rivers to the city of Truro. These usually sail from Prince of Wales Pier and Custom House Quay.

Owing to the rapid rise and fall of the tide there is not usually time for protracted sightseeing between time of arrival and departure at Truro. More time can be gained for visiting Truro by travelling one way by boat and the other by road or rail.

The hours of sailing are advertised at the various quays.

Sea Trips.—Motor boat excursions from Falmouth to Fowey, the Manacles, Helford Passage, etc., are very popular. Inquiries should be made either at the Prince of Wales Pier, or at Custom House Quay.

Tennis.—Public courts (hard) adjoining Queen Mary Gardens, Cliff Road. Visitors are admitted to the courts of the Falmouth Club, Western Terrace.

Walking.—Falmouth is at the meeting-point of two famous walking grounds—the Lizard and the coast eastward by Mevagissey to Looe. Each of these is noted for fine cliff scenery, bold headlands, beautiful coves and bathing beaches. Those who walk from Falmouth will find in the creeks around the Fal, in Roseland and along by Helford, mile upon mile of charmingly wooded scenery with grand views of sea and river.

Yachting, as may well be imagined, is extremely popular at Falmouth. The *Royal Cornwall Yacht Club* is the local headquarters, (private for members only) of sailing in the district, and there are flourishing sailing clubs also at Flushing, St. Mawes and Mylor. Racing takes place several times a week in the summer, but the event of the season is Regatta week (in August). Between 300 and 400 boats of all types race on regatta days. There are also popular regattas at St. Mawes, Helford, Flushing and Restronguet, which generally provide good sport.

Yachting and boating men find opportunities at Falmouth which can be had at few other ports in the British Isles. Should the sea in the Bay be too heavy, or the wind too strong for pleasant sailing, the Carrick Roads afford plenty of sea-room for a cruise, and there is always the river Fal. Outside Pendennis, too, a number of places invite cruises. Porthscatho, Gerrans Bay, Gull Rock, the Dodman, and Fowey to the east; Falmouth Bay, Helford River (a dreamland to members of the Canoe Club), Coverack, Cadgwith, the Lizard, and Kynance to the west, can all be reached with the right wind in a few hours. The twists and turns of Percuil River (St. Mawes), with the maze of creeks up the Fal, would take a clever skipper more than one long summer properly to explore.

IN AND ABOUT FALMOUTH

Falmouth is a seaport and flourishing resort, 266 miles by road from London; just under 100 from Exeter, 67 from Plymouth, 11 from Truro, and 26 from Penzance. With a resident population of approximately 17,550, Falmouth is the third largest town in Cornwall. The hilly nature of the promontory gives Falmouth a great advantage over other seaport holiday resorts by providing two entirely different outlooks—to the north the busy harbour with its quays and dockyards, backed by the tree-fringed Fal; on the south a magnificent prospect of sea and cliffs unsullied by the chimneys and other less beautiful adjuncts of a seaport.

The Railway Station is near the junction of **Avenue** and **Melvill Roads**; those who arrive by road will probably enter the town by the shrub-bordered **Dracæna Avenue**, which strikes up to the right soon after passing Penryn, Melvill Road continues Dracæna Avenue and runs along the ridge to the promontory. Any of the pleasant roads to the right lead to the **Cliff Road** bordering Falmouth Bay, where are the bathing beaches and other holiday attractions. The wooded slopes of **Pendennis Point** enclose the bay to the east—the walk or drive round the Head (*see* p. 43) is probably the most interesting of its kind in England. Among the trees below the coastguard houses are the pretty **Melville Gardens.** The views through the foliage and across the blue Bay to the Lizard coast are delightful. From here one has a good view of Falmouth's sea front and pleasure beaches. Almost at one's feet is the **Castle Beach**. A few hundred yards farther west is—

Gyllyngvase Beach,

easily the most popular of the Falmouth beaches. "Beach" in Cornwall signifies sand, and Gyllyngvase is as sandy as the most captious castle-builder could desire. Between June and October the temperature of the sea off Falmouth averages a minimum of 58 degrees and a maximum of 60 degrees. There are numerous bathing chalets, a beach café and shops; at the back of the beach is a large **Car Park,** and adjoining it are the **Queen Mary Gardens,** with a miniature golf course near by and other facilities for amusement and many a chair in which to lounge and enjoy the lovely view eastward—in the foreground the merry crowd of bathers on Gyllyngvase Beach and across the bay the shimmering trees covering Pendennis.

In the centre of the sea front are the—

Gyllyngdune Gardens

(Open daily 8 a.m. to dusk. Admission free.)

These gardens are one of Falmouth's surprises, for the matter-of-fact entrance gate gives no hint of the luxuriance of the vegetation within, much of which is of tropical origin.

Just within the gate is a deep grotto, or rockery (entered by a short tunnel under the roots of a big tree), with magnificent ferns. In the centre is a fine example of a New Zealand Tree Fern. This actual specimen was transported to Wembley years ago and planted in front of the New Zealand pavilion at the British Empire Exhibition. On the higher ground is the Bandstand, surrounded by a fine lawn, with a glass-covered veranda running along two sides, with many seats—a very sheltered spot on a windy day. The **Princess Pavilion** is used for concerts and other entertainments. The shady paths are bordered by beds of flowers of remarkable variety and luxuriance. Flower-lovers should not miss the greenhouses and their contents which at most times of the year present a riot of colour.

Opposite the entrance to Gyllyngdune Gardens on the sea front, is the *Chapel of Gyllyngdune House*, built by the Rev. W. J. Coope, Rector of Falmouth 1838–70.

Kimberley Park, near the Recreation Ground is a fine 7 acre expanse of open grass and park land with a paddling pool and a children's playground. For those interested in horticulture, Falmouth is indeed a continual delight, almost every garden exhibiting some plant or tree of unusual interest. The grounds of the Fox Rosehill Gardens, open on week-days, have produced marvels, winning the Banksian medal for acclimatising over two hundred species of foreign plants. At *Rose Hill* are abutilons 20 feet high, tobacco plants 14 feet, and daturas with a diameter of 15 feet. These facts offer further proof of the unique *equability* of Falmouth's climate. Another place of great horticultural interest is **Penjerrick** (*see* p. 51).

Until recently Falmouth's sea-front definitely ended at the Queen Mary Gardens, but during recent years the little beach **at Swanpool,** a little farther round the Bay, has come to be regarded by holiday-makers as part of the town. There is a large car park and a boating pool, a refreshment kiosk, while on the hill overlooking the beach is a pleasant café. Buses run to and fro during the day, passing Swanpool, but many visitors prefer the walk outlined on p. 47.

The Town

Though its streets are narrow and very full of traffic during the season, and though it has few buildings with any architectural pretensions, Falmouth town is full of interest. Walking along the main street, which under various names runs within a few yards of the water from Greenbank to the vicinity of the Outer Harbour docks, one is frequently surprised by glimpses, through doorways or between buildings, of the Harbour and its multifarious shipping. Many of the shops, too, are of a kind unfamiliar to those coming from inland cities, and generally one has that satisfying sensation of being in a place which is different. The traffic centre of Falmouth is the large open space known as **The Moor**, formerly a marsh. Here is the terminus of most of the bus and coach routes, and, as already mentioned, a handy Car Park.

At the foot of The Moor are The Municipal Buildings, the Police Court and County Court (occupying the old Town Hall) and a large block housing the **Municipal Offices** and **Council Chamber** and the **Public Library.**

The lending library comprises over 25,000 volumes; the very extensive reference libraries another 15,000, including 1,000 volumes dealing with the history of Falmouth and Cornwall. The collection of books relating to Cornwall is probably the best in the country. (*The Lending Library is open daily from* 10 *a.m. to* 8 *p.m. Reading and Magazine Room from* 9 *a.m. until* 8 *p.m. Closes Wednesdays at* 6 *p.m. and Saturdays* 1 *p.m.*). Here, too, are a number of drawings by Old Masters and oil- and water-colour paintings by more modern eminent artists, given by Mr. A. A. de Pass, whose munificence has also made it possible to enlarge the building. The **Council Chamber** contains some interesting ancient documents dealing with old Falmouth.

The striking **Post Office** building suggests somewhat invidious comparisons between the architectural styles of this corner of The Moor.

From this point it will be seen that the hilly promontory on the side of which old Falmouth lies is divided by a gorge with steep sides, covered with houses.

The hillside opposite the Post Office is scaled by a precipitous flight of 111 stone steps, called **Jacob's Ladder.** Those who climb the northern side of the valley should visit **Beacon Hill** (*see* our plan) for the sake of the view.

Near the foot of The Moor is the **Prince of Wales Pier,** from which most of the excursion steamers start and several of the ferries. Though intended as a landing stage rather than a promenade pier, it is a fine point from which to enjoy the ever-changing views of the Harbour—boats of all kinds, some at anchor, some fussily making their way in or out of the anchorage, but all with a beauty that is heightened by the background of green woods and distant hills.

South-eastward along the main street are the headquarters of the Royal Cornwall Polytechnic Society. A little farther south is—

The Parish Church

Erected in 1662–5, it is dedicated "to the memory of Charles I, King and Martyr." The pulpit is made up of various old pieces of carving. In the vestry is an old painted alabaster tablet. The church contains a portrait of the martyred King and a memorial window with figures of the King, Archbishop Laud, Bishop Juxon, etc. A tablet placed by the Burns Federation at Kilmarnock commemorates the fourteenth Earl Glencairn, friend and benefactor of Robert Burns, who died at sea when on a voyage from Lisbon to Scotland and was buried in the church. The registers date from 1663. The church maintains a tradition of congregational singing led by an excellent choir which draws a large congregation from far and wide. The Sunday morning matins are extremely popular with visitors during the summer months.

A curiosity at the entrance to the **Custom House Quay** is *The King's Pipe*, a furnace and chimney in which excise officers used to burn contraband tobacco. On the Quay is a handy Car Park. Beyond this point the road becomes open on the east, and one has more frequent glimpses of the life of the Harbour.

In a small enclosure is the **Killigrew Monument**, erected by Martin Killigrew in 1737, and recalling the ancient family for so many hundred years closely identified with the fortunes of Falmouth. The John Killigrew who died in 1576 built one of the finest mansions in Cornwall, which, however, perished during the Civil War.

The way in which John Killigrew, early in the seventeenth century, helped Falmouth into existence has already been related (*see* pp. 28–9). In 1661 Peter Killigrew was created a baronet, but the title became extinct in 1704.

In the nature of things **Docks** are seldom beautiful, and with so much that is beautiful on every hand Falmouth Docks must perforce be regarded from a utilitarian standpoint. Since their inauguration about 1860 many extensions and alterations have been made, and the work of enlarging one of the dry docks to accommodate tankers up to 90,000 tons deadweight was completed in September 1958. This dock is 850 feet long and 130 feet wide. It was named the "Queen Elizabeth Dock" by H.R.H. Prince Philip, Duke of Edinburgh, K.G., when he inspected the installation in May, 1958.

By turning right and then left under the railway bridge near the Docks one can rapidly reach the shores of Falmouth Bay, but a far better introduction is to turn to the left and follow the Castle Drive as it climbs and winds its way round Pendennis Headland (p. 43). The journey should be made at least twice—once in each direction, and it should also be made at different times of day, for the changing light makes remarkable differences in the views. From the Castle Drive the view down to the Docks is exceptionally interesting.

Pendennis Castle

Open to public Mar., April, Oct.: Weekdays, 9.30–5.30, Sundays, 2–5.30. May–Sept.: 9.30–7 (Sundays 2–7). Nov.–Feb.: Weekdays, 9.30–4, Sundays, 2–4. **Admission**, fee.
Motorists visiting castle may park their cars (free) within the precincts.

The promontory known as Pendennis Point divides the Harbour from the Bay. On the summit, about 200 feet above sea level, stands **Pendennis Castle.**

Henry VIII followed the example of several predecessors when, about 1543, he built the nucleus of the present Castle on the site of an ancient fort. The King's scheme of defence included Pendennis and St. Mawes Castles, a castle at Trefusis Point, and another between Gyllyngdune and Gyllyngvase, but the last two were not built.

Tonkin, the historian, wrote in 1730: "Queen Elizabeth raised the new fort and bettered the old fortifications, so that it may be reckoned one of the most impregnable garrisons in the kingdom."

Though Falmouth was so far from the principal centres of activity in the Civil War, Pendennis has a notable record in connection with the strife.

In 1644 Queen Henrietta Maria embarked from Pendennis for France. Prince Charles, driven westward to Bristol, and then on to Barnstaple, left Devon for Cornwall in 1645, finding refuge at Pendennis. He soon fled to Scilly. In March 1646 the Castle was besieged, both by land and sea, by the forces of the Parliament, commanded by Colonel Fortescue and Captain Batten. It was ably and stubbornly defended by Sir John Arundell, a veteran of seventy years. In the words of Lord Clarendon: "The castle refused all summons, admitting no treaty, till they had not victual for twenty-four hours, when they carried on the treaty with such firmness that their situation was never suspected, and they obtained as good terms as any garrison in England." The siege lasted about five months. Pendennis was one of the last castles to hold out for the King.

The building is admirably cared for by the Department of the Environment, but is of chief interest as a view-point—over Falmouth to the hilly country towards Redruth and Helston, and far down the eastern coast of the Lizard; over the Harbour with its marvellously coloured enclosing hills—far out to sea, where the big ships go by. Almost due east from Pendennis Point is the white lighthouse at St. Anthony (*see* p. 44), to the left of which are St. Mawes and the Percuil River; away to the north-west extends the lovely Fal.

The Castle Drive

encircling Pendennis is a most interesting road skirting the Bay on one side and the Harbour on the other. Could Falmouth offer no other attraction she would still be richer in scenery than most other seaside resorts. Along the Drive and around the Head are attractive flower gardens.

It is much more satisfying to walk round Pendennis than to drive, for it enables one to explore beyond the beaten track. Beyond the Castle lane, is *Hunter's Path*, leading up to the high ground of Pendennis. Through the foliage there are delightful views along the sea-front and down the eastern side of the Lizard, as far as the Manacles. About midway, also on the Bay side, is a little "blowing hole" in the rocks; it is small, and only noticeable at certain states of the tide. Almost at the extremity of Pendennis, still on the Bay side, is a spacious and lofty **Cave**, with a splendid entrance arch, fringed with *Asplenium marinum* ferns. At the farther end of this large cave, which is about 150 feet long, a small passage leads up to Pendennis Castle. It is said that on more than one occasion eminent persons have used this means of escape. The cave is now blocked at the seaward end to reduce erosion by the sea which was undermining the road.

Just below the car park on Pendennis Head is a Coast-guard Station, the district headquarters for all south-west Cornwall.

Falmouth Harbour and the Fal

Falmouth Harbour, the estuary of the river Fal, occupies an area of approximately 10 square miles and is one of the largest havens in the Commonwealth. The entrance from the sea is stately and imposing. On the west is the bold promontory of **Pendennis,** 200 feet high, crowned with Pendennis Castle. To the east is **St. Anthony Head,** 240 feet high, with the gleaming white Lighthouse at its foot, and then, just beyond the pretty estuary of the *Percuil River* comes St. Mawes with its castle.

The municipal authorities of Truro once exercised jurisdiction over the whole of Falmouth Harbour, a privilege said to have been granted by King John long before Falmouth (or Smithicke) was thought of. In 1703 the validity of this ancient grant was contested, and Falmouth was declared to have undisputed sway over its own harbour. The Falmouth Harbour Commissioners, formed in 1870, have jurisdiction over the broad waters of the Carrick Roads as far as an imaginary line drawn from two posts north of Messack Point to an obelisk on the opposite shore. In Falmouth Bay their authority extends as far south as Rosemullion Point.

A Cruise Round the Harbour

is the favourite and the most enjoyable way of obtaining some idea of this noble expanse. Motor boats are available. The ferry boats linking Falmouth with Flushing, St. Mawes, and other points afford opportunities for picnics and a closer examination of certain points than is possible in the course of a cruise. The Inner Harbour and docks are usually crowded with craft of all shapes and sizes, British and foreign.

The visitor may notice that many fishing boats and similar small vessels, to be seen in and about the Harbour, have big, white letters painted on their bows, followed by numbers. The letters indicate the port at which the vessel is registered and the figures the official number of the craft. Registration letters for Cornish ports are: FH = Falmouth, SS = St. Ives, PW = Padstow, PZ = Penzance, FW = Fowey, TO = Truro.

We soon face the sea, and cross the wide harbour-mouth to St. Anthony. Half-way across is the **Black Rock,** covered at high tide. For many years the Killigrew family were under obligation to keep fixed thereon a tall pole. Later this duty devolved on the parish church which received a due of 1*s*. from every ship entering the port to pay the expense of upkeep. In 1835, however, Trinity House built on the rock the granite cone, and set up the vertical standard and ball, which has a height of 36 feet. A vague tradition has it that the Phoenicians first bartered for Cornish tin on this rock.

The white **St. Anthony Lighthouse** makes a striking contrast with the mass of black rock and green hills behind.

Northward of the lighthouse the wide mouth of the Percuil River at St. Mawes opens out, with the sunny little town of **St. Mawes** on the farther side, its Castle trying to look as important as it was in the time of Henry VIII. About a mile up the winding river forming St. Mawes Harbour is **Percuil,** a pretty hamlet to which the ferries run. The wide extent of water between St. Mawes and Pill Point (over 3 miles long by 1¼ miles wide) is known as the **Carrick Roads,** where large vessels can always find a deep and safe anchorage at all states of the tide.

St. Just Pool, not very extensive, but with charmingly wooded scenery, is on our right, and a prettier creek could hardly be conceived. Some years ago a proposal was made to construct large docks for ocean liners at St. Just, but happily for the beauty of the spot the scheme fell through (*see* p. 30).

The Harbour hereabouts looks like a vast lake, with **Feock** and Porthgwidden charmingly placed among trees near the north-west shore. Away to the right, as we turn to pass down the western side, the Fal flows out from between the beautifully-wooded hills. Restronguet Point overlooks the entrance to **Restronguet Creek,** a delightful spot, extending a long distance, and including in its northern corner **Penpoll Creek** and to the north-west, the once busy little port of **Devoran.** Boating parties should keep a keen eye on tide and channel, as there is not much water here at low tide. A mile farther south is **Mylor Creek** (between the trees we can distinguish Mylor Church, close to the water), also with pleasures and penalties for boaters;

and then as **Trefusis Point** is rounded Falmouth comes fully into view. On the right is the **Penryn River,** a branch of the Harbour extending for 3 miles to Penryn. Sheltering snugly under Trefusis is the little town of **Flushing,** one of the most sheltered corners in England and much frequented by invalids suffering from chest complaints.

THE RIVER FAL

We have already referred to the popularity of the trips on the river Fal. The beauty of the river, with its numberless creeks, cannot be described, nor can it be fully appreciated from a fast-moving motor boat. It is essentially a waterway in which to "potter," though the tides must be carefully watched (especially in the creeks). Here we can indicate only the features of special interest between Carrick Roads and Truro.

Straight ahead from where the river narrows is Trelissick (*National Trust*), a mansion with gardens noted for their almost tropical luxuriance. (*Grounds open to visitors on weekdays and Bank Holiday Mondays from March to October,* 11–6 *Sundays,* 2–6 *Admission charge.*) The waters narrow further, and we are in the most beautiful reach of the river. **King Harry Passage** is lovely at all times. A ferry (carrying cars, etc.: *see* p. 34) connects the roads on either hand. Various little creeks lead off on the left. The arm on the right is the **Fal,** navigable for 3 miles to Ruan. Between the Fal and the **Truro River** is Lord Falmouth's estate, **Tregothnan.** Tregothnan boathouse will be seen at the foot of the hill, almost covered by overhanging trees.

Continuing by the Truro River, in about 2 miles we reach the *Park Hotel* at **Malpas** (pronounced Mopus). The Tresillian River branches to the right, and here at certain states of the tide the boats turn back and passengers for Truro land at Malpas and complete the journey (2 miles) by bus or afoot. If the tide serves, however, the vessels go up to the centre of the city, providing one of the best distant views of the Cathedral. The last part of the course is very tortuous.

Truro is described on pp. 81–86.

The Falmouth District

Falmouth is such an excellent centre and a recognised starting point for so many famous excursions that the attractions of the immediate neighbourhood are apt to be overlooked. For reasons which should be obvious we think it best to mention only a few of the many pleasant walks near at hand; those not averse to taking a friendly hint will study a map with the aid of ferry and bus time-tables.

I. SWANPOOL AND MAENPORTH

Swanpool and Maenporth are popular bathing and picnic resorts. Numerous buses from Falmouth. Refreshment places.

Road Route.—From Gyllyngvase Beach go westward by Spernan Wyn Road and keep straight on at cross-roads, shortly descending past the Cemetery to Swanpool lake and beach. There is no way round by Boscawen Road or Hangman Hill. For Maenporth continue past Swanpool and turn left at Golden Bank cross-roads beyond Golf Links.

These two places may be included in a walk of about 6 miles. If the whole distance is too great, bus can be used. At the top of Killigrew Road bear left and first right into Marlborough Avenue. At *Marlborough House* turn left, passing the house on the right, and follow the avenue to Swanpool Hill which leads in a south-westerly direction to the main road near **Swanpool,** a large reed-fringed lake. The pool is separated from the sea only by the road, and the very popular beach is of shingle and sand. There is a refreshment kiosk on the beach and a café beside the road leading up to the **Golf Links.** Just beyond the café a path on the left strikes off across Pennance Point and runs within sight of the sea all the way to Maenporth.

Maenporth, a pretty little sandy cove with cliffs worn into caves and arches, together with an underground stream which flows on to the beach, is a popular picnic resort. Refreshments can be obtained at a café on the beach.

Two and three-quarter miles south-west is **Helford Passage** (*Ferry Boat Inn*)—the estuary of the lovely Helford River, where it makes its placid exit to the sea. The buses run through Maenporth to Mawnan Smith and Trebah (for Helford Passage). Other services run from Falmouth to Constantine and villages on the northern shore, and for those indisposed to an immediate return to Falmouth, the lanes in this quiet corner offer endless possibilities (*see* also p. 50).

II. FLUSHING, TREFUSIS AND MYLOR

A circular walk of about 4 miles, which is a good introduction to characteristic Fal scenery. The ferry from Prince of Wales Pier brings us across the Inner Harbour to—

Flushing,

a warm and sunny little village. Dutch families are said to have founded a small settlement here long before Falmouth came into being. They called it Flushing after the Dutch port of that name. During the stirring and flourishing days when the Falmouth Packets were in operation, the quay was gay with the uniforms of the officers, many of whom, with their wives and families, resided in this pleasant and rather select corner of Falmouth Harbour. Today, Flushing has lapsed into a quiet and dignified riverside village with fine views across the Harbour and strong claims as a centre for grand walks in all directions. The main inner quay is used by ferries plying to and from Falmouth. Close to the door of St. Peter's Church is the remnant of a Cornish cross. At **Little Falmouth,** to the north of Flushing, several of the packets were built.

Turn to the right on leaving Flushing quay, the road leading pleasantly round, past a few private houses, and so to the woods of **Trefusis,** or to the beach to the right.

Cars are not allowed to continue beyond the houses, but the footpath continues right round the point, northward through the fields (or there is a shorter approach straight up through Flushing village and across the fields) to—

Mylor,

once the site of a royal dockyard, the smallest in Great Britain, now in use as a boat repair yard and yacht harbour. Here too

Porthscatho

Mullion Cove

Gunwalloe Cove

Kynance Cove

is a popular yacht haven. The hamlet overlooks a wide inlet at the mouth of the creek which runs up to the village of **Mylor Bridge**.

Beside the south door of **Mylor Church** is the largest and tallest Cornish cross extant, probably fashioned by early Celtic missionaries. It was discovered in 1870, head downward, serving as a prop for the south wall of the church. It is of granite, 17 feet 6 inches high, with a round head. The present position does not set off its height to advantage, as the lower portion is embedded 7 feet. St. Mylor (*c.* 450), was a Celtic bishop who is also the patron saint of Tremeloir near St. Brieuc in Brittany. Notice the fine Norman doorways, one in the north wall of the Church, the other on the west side, and the thirteenth-century carving of the Crucifixion in the outer recess on the north side of the chancel. The font is thirteenth century; the pulpit Elizabethan. The church displays the arms of Charles I and Queen Anne and a copy of Charles' famous letter. A grave-stone in the churchyard, near the east window, bears the following inscription:

In
memory of mr
Joseph Crapp-ship
wright who died ye 26th of
Novbr 1770 Aged 43 years
Alafs Frend Joseph
His End wor Allmost Sudden
As thou the mandate came
Exprefs from heaven
his foot it Slip And he did fall
help help he cries & that was all.

To the right by the fork in the path is another stone commemorating Thomas James, a smuggler shot by a customs officer:

"Officious zeal in luckless hour laid wait
And wilful sent the murderous ball of fate."

Flushing may be regained by the road above the west gate of the churchyard, or there is a more pleasant path across the fields, to the left of the road.

III. ST. BUDOCK CHURCH

About 2 miles in a westerly direction. Follow Tregenver Road, by the side of the Recreation Ground, for a hundred yards, then go down the hill on the left past the suburb at *Swanvale*. Then take a pathway on the right across the fields; it leads up to **St. Budock Church,** on the hill. There are several alternative paths. It is a pleasant round to go to Budock *via* Swanpool, and back by the field-path which abuts on Trescobeas road.

St. Budocus, Bishop of Dol, lived in the sixth century. Another saint of the same name was a prince of Cornwall, and lived A.D. 500. The church, with its ancient screen (restored), bespeaks its age. Note the painted panels representing saints. The brass of John Killigrew, of Arwenack, *ob.* 1567, is good. There are effigies of John Killigrew and his wife, and a monument to Sir Nicholas Parker (1619). The registers date from 1653. The church has Georgian Box pews.

IV. MAWNAN AND HELFORD PASSAGE

By cliff-path to **Maenporth,** as in Route I. About a mile farther, on level high ground, turn to the left for the church of **Mawnan,** very delightfully situated, with extensive views. Note the fourteenth-century north aisle windows, the remains of the painted rood-screen and the fifteenth-century font. The seventeenth-century shelf alms-box has the inscription: "Remember the Poore."

Mawnan Smith village (*Red Lion Inn*), a mile north-west, is becoming popular with those who like country quarters near to the sea. There are facilities for bowls, and buses keep the village in close touch with Falmouth.

From Mawnan Smith a road goes south-west *via* the hamlet of Trebah, to **Helford Passage** (*Ferry Boat Inn*), with its pleasant little beach beside the Helford river which is popular with boating and fishing folk. Those with an explorative nature should turn down some of the lanes in this lovely corner—that to **Durgan,** for example (on left, a mile short of Helford Passage), passes through woods overhanging the estuary and suddenly and most charmingly reveals the little hamlet at the foot of the wooded cliffs. There is a pedestrian ferry between Helford Passage and Helford during summer.

V. PENJERRICK

Although the distance by road is only 3 miles, the route is rather difficult for a stranger to find. Proceed by way of Marlborough Avenue and Golden Bank, thence across fields to Lower Crill, turn to left and keep straight on. The return can be made *via* Budock Water and Budock Church.

Penjerrick, with its lovely grounds, should certainly be visited. (*Bus to the gate from Falmouth Moor.*) The public are admitted to the grounds *daily* 2–4.30, *March to September. Collection box.* Only a botanist's pen can do justice to these beautiful and wonderful grounds. Whatever it is possible to grow in England is grown here. The gardens have been laid out with a cunning art that conceals art, and the view down the valley to the sea is glorious. Each shrub and plant is of interest either for its size, its luxuriance of growth, its unusual flowering capability, or its acclimatisation in England. The collections of rhododendrons, azaleas and camellias are particularly fine in Spring.

VI. PENRYN

Early Closing.—Thursdays.
Hotels.—*King's Arms, Anchor, The Penrynian.*
Railway Station.—On the Falmouth branch line. The station stands in the highest part of the town. Tel.: Penryn 3122.
Bus Services.—Daily to Falmouth, Helston and Truro, Redruth, etc.
Market Day.—Saturday.

Penryn, long famous for its granite, stands at the head of the river on which Falmouth old town is built, and although the quays are still generally busy with shipping there was a time (*see* p. 28) when Penryn was the predominant port in these parts. **The Green,** near the Quay, has a public bowling green. In the Town Hall are the old stocks. A museum in the Market Place shows a horse-drawn fire engine and other items of local interest.

The few remains of **Glasney Collegiate Church,** erected at Penryn in the thirteenth century, are of archæological interest. Founded by Bishop Bronescombe the church served as an important centre of ecclesiastical learning for over 300 years.

In the northern part of the town, and near the river, is **St. Gluvias Church,** with a fifteenth-century granite tower. Within is a brass with figures of Thomas Kyllgrewe and his wives—1489.

Cornish historians are reluctant to assign a birthday to Penryn. Domesday Book records its existence. James I and II gave charters to the town following the first Bishop's Charter in 1236. In early days two small piers, one on each side of Penryn Creek, were connected by a swing bridge.

The pretty **College Woods** close to Penryn Station are a favourite picnic resort. Ferns grow here in profusion, and during springtime few places round Falmouth are more gorgeously decked with primroses and bluebells. The woods take their name from the scanty remains of *Glasney College* (*see* above).

About half a mile from the centre of Penryn, on the Helston road, stands *Tremough*—a convent boarding-school for girls—having in its grounds the most representative collection of Himalayan rhododendrons in the British Isles—many are over 30 feet high. Camellias are to be seen here 20 feet in height.

VII. CONSTANTINE

Inn.—*Queen's Arms.*
Bus Service to and from Falmouth (7 miles) Helston and Redruth.

This large parish, about 7 miles south-west of Falmouth, has the distinction of being one of the prettiest in Cornwall. **Constantine** is close to the head of the lovely Helford River, loftily placed on granite hills and surrounded by valleys, woods and streams. There are splendid facilities for sailing and fishing on sheltered waters of river and creeks, while the diversity of the scenery gives to the whole neighbourhood exceptional charm. There are many ancient footpaths, enabling this fascinating and varied countryside to be safely explored on foot. The village of Constantine has good shops, and a typically Cornish 'Churchtown', or square of well maintained cottages beside the very beautiful church. Waterside scenery at Port Navas, Helford Passage and quaintly-named Gweek (part of the latter only is in the parish) should not be missed.

The church, whose list of vicars dates from 1258, although the present handsome building is 15th century, is dedicated to St. Constantine, a one-time warrior king of Cornwall. The earlier tower of three bells were in 1958 added to, so that the fine tower now has a peal of six. A noteworthy brass is one to the memory of Richard Gerveys and Jane (Trefusys) his wife, engraved with their effigies and those of their eight boys and eight girls. It is dated 1574. This is a palimpsest brass, with the earlier figure of a knight engraved into its reverse side. Over many years, members of the church have embroidered a splendid collection of kneelers, in designs of local interest.

The curious **Piskey Hall** will be found in a field on the right, a little way out of Constantine opposite **Trewardreva.** The *History of Cornwall* describes it as "a subterranean passage, about 30 feet long, 5 feet wide, and 6 feet high. The walls and coverings are of unwrought granite. Its use has not been ascertained." Formerly the entrance was small.

Roseland

Buses from Truro and St. Austell to St. Mawes, Porthscatho, etc.

Various craft, motor and sail, ply from Falmouth to St. Mawes and Percuil, St. Anthony, St. Just, etc.

There is a footpath along the coast between St. Just and St. Mawes.

Roseland is the name given to the charming country bordering the eastern side of Carrick Roads, bounded roughly on the north by the river Fal from Ruan and extending southwards to the tip of the peninsula at Zoze Point. The name Roseland has no origin in roses but is a later form of "Rosinis" meaning "moorland isle" and Roseland very nearly is an island. Far from railways and with numerous winding creeks tending to isolate little districts still more both from each other and from the outside world, it is a splendid area for walkers and for those motorists who are not averse to narrow, winding lanes. The two chief centres of population are St. Mawes and Porthscatho; but almost equally popular are the various little hamlets, and during the season accommodation is usually rather difficult to obtain.

There is a caravan site and several bed and breakfast signs. The area has great charm and an increasing popularity. Skin-diving, water-skiing and motor-boating are great attractions from the beaches.

The narrow promontory facing St. Mawes and terminating in Zoze Point is well worth exploration. Boats from Falmouth call at St. Mawes and cross to the little landing-place opposite *Place Manor Hotel*, which as a charmingly situated mansion was built by Admiral Spry over the remains of a Priory.

The second gate on the right leads to the Church of **St. Anthony-in-Roseland.** (The key is obtained at *Place.*) This Church contains some fine examples of Early English architecture. Notice the lights in the little steeple. The south door has a pre-Norman arch, and the nave is mainly Norman. Here was a small priory connected with the Austin Priory at Plympton. The conventual part of the Church was rebuilt in 1259. The registers date from 1660.

For **St. Anthony Lighthouse** walk or drive to the end of the military road (¾ m.) overlooking Carrick Roads and take the path through gate on *right*. The light is a sector light, showing white and red sectors, the red sector marking the Manacles rocks. The occulting light shows for seventeen seconds and is then eclipsed for three seconds. It is visible 13 miles. The horn outside the lantern is used in fog. The bell originally in use weighed two tons and has now been given to a Falmouth church. The lighthouse may be visited on weekday afternoons. Another approach is through the National Trust car park and down pathway on the right.

The view over Falmouth Harbour from the high ground above the Lighthouse is very fine and on a clear day extends far down the Lizard and up beyond Truro. It is particularly beautiful at sundown, when the mysterious dusk of the waterways is broken by the twinkling yellow and coloured lights of the shipping.

There is a little bathing beach a short distance north of the Lighthouse, and a stile in the lane a few hundred yards beyond its meeting with the road up from the *Place Manor Hotel* indicates another way down to the shore.

The cliffs above the Lighthouse are within the care of the National Trust (car park), and can be followed eastward to Porthscatho, passing two small beaches, Porthbeor and Towan (*car park*), reached respectively from Bohortha and Porth Farm. The road, however, is very pretty and has at least equal claim. It joins the road up from Percuil a little short of **Gerrans**

(*Royal Standard Inn*), a pleasant village with good views over Gull Rock and Nare Head.

The Church appears very ancient, but it was practically rebuilt in 1848. The font is Norman; the granite piers supporting the arches are fifteenth century, as is also the spire, which was repaired in 1636 and again in 1890. There is a holy-water stoup in the south porch, and outside is a Celtic cross. The old bench-ends in the front pews deserve notice. The registers date from 1538. The church is dedicated to Gerennius, a king of Cornwall, afterwards canonized.

St. Mawes,

Early Closing.—Thursday.
Car Park.—On Quay, the Square.
Hotels.—*Ship and Castle; St. Mawes; Tresanton; Idle Rocks; Rising Sun; Victory Inn; Manor; Mount; Polvarth Guest House; Pen-Eglos Guest House.*
Licensing Hours.—11–2 and 6–11. Sundays, 12–2 and 7–10.30.

on the western shore of the promontory, may be regarded as the "capital" of Roseland. Built up in terraces rising from the Harbour, the situation of this little port, holiday resort and former Parliamentary borough, is undeniably fine, and it is not surprising that the place is flourishing. It is well protected from both north and south, has a splendid view of the mouth of Falmouth Harbour and of the open sea, and enjoys the maximum of sunshine. Several of the ancient and picturesque houses and cottages offer holiday accommodation which is snapped up very early. There are several hotels. On the eastern side of the miniature bay are some fine modern residences. Communication with the outer world is maintained by the ferry to Falmouth and a bus service to and from Truro.

Pleasant as St. Mawes is, the views from it are even more delightful. It is a grand place for sailing and boating of all kinds, and the harbour, the beach, and the Percuil river alone will provide endless opportunities for short-range exploration.

St. Mawes Castle, contemporary with Pendennis Castle across the water, is commanded by hills, and when held for Charles I could not long defy the Parliament. It was built 1540–3 as part of Henry VIII's programme of coastal defence and designed purely as an artillery fort to protect Falmouth Haven with the aid of the guns of Pendennis Castle. There are fine inscriptions in praise of Henry VIII and Edward VI. The Castle is in the care of the Department of the Environment. (*Open weekdays, March to April,* 9.30–5.30, *May to September*, 9.30–7, *Oct.* 9.30–5.30, *November to February*, 9.30–4. *Sundays in summer*, 9.30–7, *otherwise from* 2 *p.m. Admission charge.*) There is a car park, free to visitors.

About a dozen yards above the *Victory Inn*, and at the top of the steps in the road, is a **Holy Well** (believed to be mainly fifteenth century), which, having fallen into disrepair, was restored and reconditioned in 1939.

St. Mawe. St. Maudite, St. Mat, St. Mawe, St. Machu, St. Machutus, and St. Maclovius appear to be one and the same person, whom we now recognise by the name of St. Mawe. He was a Welsh saint, and subsequently a prelate of St. Bretagne. "The existence of a well, combined with the solitariness of the site, and with the warmth of the rocky bank facing the noonday sun, seemed to invite his settlement at this particular ground. There he lived as a hermit; forming himself a chair in the rock above the well for the enjoyment of the warm situation." (*Ancient and Holy Wells.*)

St. Mawes Harbour is formed by the small but pretty river which comes down from beyond **Percuil** (pronounced with a hard *c*), still sometimes known by its old name, Porthcuel. A ferry calls from Falmouth.

Porthscatho

Buses from Truro *via* Tregony.

Boat communication with Falmouth *via* Percuil.

Hotels.—*Eshcol House, Rosevine, Roseland House, Gerrans Bay.*

Inns.—*Plume of Feathers* and *Standard.* **Early Closing.**—*Wednesday.*

Guest Houses.—*Tregerein, Pengerrans, Clifton, etc.*

Formerly a quiet little fishing village which has become very popular with those who enjoy a holiday having for its amusements such simple joys as fishing, boating and bathing. There are two inns, hotel and bed and breakfast facilities. Porthscatho is rather more bracing than many places along this coast, since it faces east and is not wedged in between high hills. Formerly the village was very dependent upon the fishing industry, considerable catches being made from time to time, but the boats sheltering behind the breakwater are mostly for pleasure trips. The views across Gerrans Bay extend past the isolated **Gull Rock** and **Nare Head** (*National Trust*) to **Dodman Point,** off Mevagissey.

By Tregassa and three miles of lovely lanes one can cross to the western shore of Roseland at—

St. Just-in-Roseland

two miles north of St. Mawes, it is reached by road, *via* the King Harry Ferry, from the west. It is a pretty village but its chief attraction is the famous Churchyard and the Church.

The **Church** chancel dates from 1261; the rest, including the tower, is fifteenth century. The tower contains three bells, the oldest being the tenor, originally hung in 1684 and bearing the names of two Church wardens, a small figure of Charles II and two copper coins of the period. The site is much earlier and a church was probably founded by Celtic missionaries around A.D. 550. Attention is directed to the porch and windows, the carved bench-ends, the fifteenth-century font, a fine brass of a priest and the double piscina. The chancel has been restored, the Victorian tiles on the floor being replaced with Cornish stone.

The churchyard, which is visited annually by many thousands of people from all over the country, is exceptionally lovely. With its overhanging trees, sub-tropical plants and flowering shrubs it is perched, precariously, on the sides of a steep, well-wooded hill. There are two lych-gates. From that on the road above the churchyard a beautiful prospect is unfolded. The church is seen down below, beside the creek, charmingly situated amid rich green foliage, while beyond, between the trees, are glimpses of the waters of St. Just Creek. The other lych-gate (sometimes missed by visitors), lies on the edge of the water, behind the church. The best time to visit this very beautiful spot is at high tide.

FALMOUTH TO ST. AUSTELL BY THE COAST

There has been considerable improvement of the cliff path immediately above St. Anthony Lighthouse, thus opening the way for an almost uninterrupted cliff walk all the way to Mevagissey.

This route along the cliffs, sometimes by road, more often by rough path, should be attempted only by those used to hard walking. Various fishing villages are tucked away in narrow gorges in the cliffs, and are welcome havens of rest after a spell of arduous tramping. Buses run down to one or two of the coast villages from Truro and St. Austell, but some of the services are very infrequent.

From the cliffs on either side of Porthscatho **Gerrans Bay** makes an imposing sweep, completed by Nare Head, with the Gull Rock just outside and the Dodman looming beyond. The path continues round the bay by **Pendower Beach,** nearly a mile in length. (Hotel accommodation—*Pendower Hotel.*) Bathing may be had here, anemones flourishing among the rocks, and there is a great variety of shells. Pendower is popular with picnickers.

Near the eastern end of the beach, which terminates in the conspicuous promontory of **Nare Head** (331 ft.) (*National Trust*), is the *Nare Hotel,* and on high ground above is **Carne Beacon,** a mound 370 feet in circumference. According to tradition, this was the burial-place of Gerennius, Cornish saint and king (*circa* 600), whose castle and palace stood at Dingerein, an earthwork between Carne and Gerrans. A pretty story was related in connection with his burial, somewhat reminding one of Lohengrin's death. The body of the king was conveyed in a golden boat with silver oars across Gerrans Bay and buried, with boat and oars, in the mound. In the *Journal* of the Royal Institution of Cornwall, 1855, is a report on the excavation of the mound. A kistvaen was discovered, containing ashes, but neither golden boat nor silver oars. The summit of the Beacon commands, on a clear day, one of the finest panoramas of Mid-Cornwall. Below it and well seen from the Veryan road, is Ringarounds, another ancient earthwork.

In common with every other hamlet along the coast, Carne has its quota of summer visitors.

Veryan (*New Inn*), a mile and a half inland, is a charming Cornish village in a wooded valley. The place is noted for its "round houses," of which there are so few examples in England. Two stand at each end of the village and one in the centre, each surmounted by a cross.

There are two "holy" wells in Veryan, one in the left-hand hedge in the lane leading to Veryan green, the other opposite the lych gate outside the school. The Church, dedicated to St. Symphorian, was almost rebuilt in 1847–50, but contains some thirteenth- and fifteenth-century work. The church has recently been restored and new pews have been installed.

The attractive "Homeyard Homes," erected in 1957 were built for six widows of Cornish seamen. They contain two round houses, four bungalows and a Matron's house.

Below the church is a very pretty little garden, with lake, bridges and seats—a pleasant place in which to rest.

Half a mile at sea is the **Gull Rock** (*National Trust*). From Nare Head it is a stiff up-and-down walk of 2 miles to the delightful miniature fishing village of **Portloe** (*Lugger Hotel, Ship Inn*), in a steep valley through which a stream flows to the sea. There is good fishing and bathing in the rocky little cove. The cliff path between Portloe and West Portholland is quite strenuous but the views are very good. We then drop down to **West Portholland,** and, a little farther round the cliff road, to **East Portholland,** quaint and tiny places wedged between hills and cliffs. The valley leading down to East Portholland is prettily wooded.

The road, now near the cliffs brings us to **Porthluney Cove,** the best bathing beach between Porthscatho and Pentewan, though it is dangerous to swim near the rocks or during a receding tide. With a lovely background of trees and rhododendrons at the head of the Cove is **Caerhayes Castle.** The castle is a modern replacement (1808, by Nash) of a Tudor House which belonged to the old Cornish family of Trevanion. The little Norman Church of St. Michael Caerhayes, on the high ground behind the castle, re-dedicated in 1259, contains memorials, including the helmets of deceased warriors and a sword said to have been used by Hugh Trevanion at Bosworth.

Climbing the cliffs beyond the Cove the path rejoins the road half a mile short of Bowsinger, from which a very steep and narrow lane wriggles down to **Hemmick Beach,** on the western side of—

Dodman Point

(373 ft.), the boldest headland between Falmouth and Plymouth.

It has been the cause of many a shipwreck, even in recent years. On the summit is a tall granite *Cross,* which serves as a landmark. There is a glorious view. Dodman Point is National Trust property.

Inland is **St. Goran** (*Barley Sheaf Inn*)—or Gorran, as it is spelt when the saintly prefix is dropped—which in summer achieves some importance as the postal and "shopping" centre for visitors staying in various small neighbouring hamlets and is itself busy with visitors. There is an attractive church.

In another mile we reach **Gorran Haven,** a former fishing village now transformed into a popular resort. There is a car park close to the beach (*Llawnroc Hotel; Ismeer Hotel*). There is fishing, and the little sandy beach with its stone quay is particularly pretty, being divided by an arm of cliff, which not only imparts picturesqueness but affords protection from wind. A mile and a quarter from the shore is a group of rocks, always visible, called **Gwineas** (sometimes pronounced *Gwinges*).

From Gorran Haven the cliff path continues past Turbot Point and **Chapel Point** to **Portmellon,** a sort of overflow from Mevagissey, which is a mile beyond, by the road which here joins the cliffs. Above Chapel Point is **Bodrugan** (part of the headland is in care of the National Trust) associated with the famous Bodrugan's Leap. Here Sir Henry Bodrugan made his escape by leaping into a boat below, or so it is said: but the exact scene of this incident is not pointed out. For **Mevagissey,** *see* pp. 95–7.

The Lizard

Access.—Camborne and Redruth stations are the nearest main-line stops for the Lizard from whence there are bus connections with Helston, Mullion, Lizard Town and other points on the promontory. The rail journey from Looe, Falmouth, etc., is roundabout and involves tiresome changes. There are, however, numerous coach trips embracing the Lizard from Falmouth, Truro, Fowey, and other Cornish centres, and boats from Falmouth land passengers at Coverack.

Bathing.—Visitors should note that it is, generally speaking, dangerous to bathe near the rocky sides of a cove at any except high tide if the water is at all rough; in a strong wind the "drag" of the retreating waves is dangerous anywhere and liable to trap the strongest swimmer.

Hotels.—*Housel Bay; Caerthillian; Lizard; Polbrean; Penmenner Guest House; Kynance Bay Guest House; Parc-an-Castle Guest House.*

Motoring.—The routes to the various coves are outlined on pp. 18–19.

Some of the finest scenery of the kind in Britain is presented by the coves and cliffs both east and west of the Lizard. It is therefore small wonder that the promontory forms the most popular goal for excursions in Cornwall, with the possible exception of Land's End—and the prior claims of the Land's End must be ascribed rather to romance than to scenic grandeur, for in that respect the Lizard is incomparably finer. Here the cliffs assume not only weird shapes but marvellous colours, such as can only be matched around St. Agnes and Trevaunance Cove on the north coast.

Practically the whole of the peninsula is a tableland about 300 feet above sea-level, the highest point being at *Dry Tree* which has an elevation of 370 feet. The centre is an expansive tract called **Goonhilly Downs,** covered with the heath *Erica vagans*, familiarly known as Cornish heath, which flowers in the late summer and autumn. Throughout May and early June the Downs are a sheet of golden gorse, the scent of which is almost overpowering. Along the Helston road gorse is mingled with the snow-like blackthorn flower. The southern Downs sloping to Kynance and Caerthillian Coves are at midsummer a paradise for the botanist, especially as regards the rarer clovers and rushes. Not long since there were counted, on a casual walk from the Lizard to Kynance, no fewer than twenty-one rare plants.

In recent years the Lizard has come to be recognised as one

of the finest areas in Britain for a walking holiday. Many of the grandest cliff scenes are only accessible afoot or in a boat, and if Kynance, Mullion and other celebrated places are apt to be crowded during the day in the season, there are countless other spots of almost equal attraction which are virtually unknown to all but the enterprising rambler.

Mullion and Lizard Town are the two most popular head-quarters, but Coverack, Cadgwith and all the smaller hamlets, not excluding isolated farmhouses and cottages, have their quota of visitors. The stranger will possibly be surprised at the size of some of the more modern hotels—several of them in relatively outlying situations.

THE COAST WALK ROUND THE LIZARD

The 36-mile walk by the coast-watchers' path from Loe Pool, near Helston, to Helford, is one of the best in England, but it must be remembered that nearly every one of these miles is over ground both trying and steep, so that in drawing up an itinerary the daily stages should not be too ambitious. Needless to say, for those who like to combine walking with sketching or photography, or some form of nature study, there is enough material to justify the expenditure of a month or more in rambling from Helston to Helford. Except near the hotels and inns indicated, houses are scarce, and protection from inclement weather is not always obtainable. In places the path is fairly distinct, at others it has to be discovered by a keen sense of direction. The following alternative itineraries may be useful:

Three Days' Walk

1. Helston and Loe Pool	to Kynance	13 miles.
	or Housel Bay	16 „
2. Kynance or Housel Bay	to Coverack	13 „ / 10 „
3. Coverack to Helford		11 „

Four Days' Walk

1. Helston to Mullion (by cliffs)	7 miles.
2. Mullion to Housel Bay	8 „
3. Housel Bay to Coverack	10 „
4. Coverack to Helford	11 „

The second itinerary is the better, because it allows Mullion Cove to be visited at low water, leaving Kynance for another tide.

Roads on to the Lizard promontory pass either through the village of **Gweek** (*see* p. 80) or by—

Helston

Buses run to Helston from Falmouth, Camborne, Redruth, Penzance, etc. From Helston to Poldhu, Mullion, The Lizard, Coverack, St. Keverne, Porthallow, Manaccan, Gillan, etc.
Car Parks at west end of town and off Meneage Street.
Early Closing.—Wednesday.
Hotels.—*Angel*, Coinage Hall Street; *Alpha*, Coinage Hall Street; *Bona-Vista Guest House*, Meneage Road; *Nansloe Guest House*, Meneage Road.
Library.—County Branch Library Trengrouse Way.
Licensing Hours.—10–2.30 and 5.30–10.30. Sundays, 12–2 and 7–10.30.
Market Day.—Monday (cattle market).
Museum.—Contains an interesting collection of ancient agricultural implements and craft tools, pictures and photographs of local scenes and events, etc.
Places of Worship.—*St. Michael's (Parish) Church, Methodist Chapels.* Sunday services, 11 and 6. *R.C. Church.*
Population.—10,570.
Post Office.—Coinagehall Street. 8.30 a.m.–5.30 p.m.

Helston, by reason of its situation, its antiquity and business accommodation, is one of Cornwall's important market towns. It appears to have existed in the time of King Alfred and was long a walled city, with a castle. The earliest-known charter was granted by King John, to whom the men of Helston gave forty silver marks and a palfrey (1201). In Stuart days, when Killigrew commenced the building of Falmouth, Helston petitioned the King that the work might cease, fearing rivalry to Helston trade. Edward I created "Helleston" a coinage town for tin, and the Hall stood in Coinage Hall Street until the beginning of the nineteenth century. In 1548 the Cornish insurrection commenced at Helston, headed by Hugh Arundel, Governor of St. Michael's Mount, who was defeated at the siege of Exeter and executed.

Helston is a good centre for the tourist, with tennis courts and putting and bowling greens, while grand walks abound in the neighbourhood. It is at its most interesting, however, on May 8th, the **Flora** or **Furry Day** (possibly from the Cornish *feur*, a fair, or holiday).

Formerly the townsfolk and people from the countryside, garlanded with flowers and headed by fiddlers, danced through the streets and in and out of the houses, and this custom has been revived in a modified form. For the dancing which follows, music is furnished by the Helston Town Band. Some residents take a holiday for the great occasion. Business is forgotten for a time and traffic is brought to a standstill as the streets become ever more tightly packed with the townsfolk—reinforced by sightseers from many miles around. Flora Day at Helston is heralded by the early morning ringing of the parish church bells and the first Furry Dance usually commences at 7 a.m. At ten o'clock the children of the various schools dance through the town, and at twelve o'clock is *the* dance of the day—the last usually takes place at 5 p.m. The "Furry dance" air is widely known; once heard, it is not soon forgotten. It has been established that the festival has no Greek origin, "Flora" being therefore a mere corruption.

Still another feature is the Hal-an-Tow which with all its pageantry has been revived by the Old Cornish Society in recent years.

Another annual event is the Helston Harvest Fair, held during early September.

Nature lovers will find much of interest for otter, fox, stoat and weasel have all been seen in the district.

St. Michael's Church (p.c. 9.30) was rebuilt by Earl Godolphin in 1763. An unusual feature is the twenty-four branch chandelier, a gift from the Earl of Godolphin in 1763. The east window dedicated in 1938 includes two angels dancing the Furry Dance, the opening bars of which also appear in musical notation. Opposite the south door is the grave of Henry Trengrouse, inventor of the Rocket Life-saving Apparatus, who only perfected his great discovery after years of intensive effort and many disappointments. The visitor will notice that the inscriptions on many of the tombstones in this burial-ground are cut in exceptionally large characters, as is also the case in the churchyard at Mullion. In the church may be seen the brass effigies of one Thomas Bougins and his family, dated 1602. The church was restored and refurbished in 1972.

Sir William Treloar, Lord Mayor of London in 1906–7, who founded the Cripples' Home at Alton, was born at Helston in 1843. At the *Blue Anchor Inn*, in Coinage Hall Street, there was discovered an ancient painted ceiling. This old house dates back to the seventeenth century and there is an old skittle alley still in use.

Near the top of the hill (marked by a plaque over the doorway and a letter-box in the wall) is the cottage in which *Robert* (*Bob*) *Fitzsimmons* the famous boxer was born in 1863.

For those travelling by road, Helston is the main gateway to the Lizard.

From it runs the fine road (A3083) which forms the key to all the roads in the peninsula, and through it pass hundreds and thousands of cars, buses and coaches.

Coming from the east one turns to the left

into Clodgey Lane, keeping straight on to avoid the congestion of town traffic and bearing slightly right. At the end of Clodgey Lane, one passes a Girls' Home and the War Memorial Hospital on the right, and directly through the centre of the grounds of **Culrose Aerodrome.** This road has now become the A3083. The old road to Lizard Town is rejoined in about 2 miles. For the eastern side of the peninsula watch for turn to left for St. Keverne, etc. Follow A3083 right through for the Lizard (the most southerly town in England). Branch roads lead off to the right for Gunwalloe, Poldhu, Mullion and Kynance (Toll Road).

The north-west coast of the Lizard may be said to begin at **Porthleven,** a busy little fishing port at the head of a combe, about 3 miles from Helston. This place is just beginning to realise its potentialities as a resort for those who like quiet holidays; the fishing is first class and there is boating, bathing from the beach of rather coarse sand, and the unending interest (to townsfolk at any rate) of a harbour. On a calm day this is a beautiful corner of Mount's Bay, but winter tells a different tale. In fact, the stretch of coast between the Lizard and Land's End has been a trap for ships from the beginning of navigation. During a storm in 1912 the silt was shifted from the strand between Porthleven and Loe Bar, and so much Spanish coin was picked up that the beach became known locally as "the gold mine." Porthleven has a remarkably equable climate and the valley leading down to the village is famous for its rich growth of semi-tropical flowers.

Notwithstanding the possibilities of treasure-trove, however, walkers bound for the Lizard coast generally go direct from Helston to **Loe Pool,** a mile or so east of Porthleven.

Starting from Helston, descend to the lower part of the town and take the Porthleven road (to the left of Lower Green). On the left at the far end of the Green is a stone gate marked "Private path to Penrose." This is a beautiful walk between the hills, and leads through the grounds of *Penrose* (gates closed 8 p.m. summer, 5 p.m. winter; no dogs, even if led; cars, cycles are prohibited.

Loe Pool, about 2 miles long, the largest lake in Cornwall, is now in sight, and makes a beautiful picture, with the thickly-wooded hills mirrored on its surface. Tennyson is said to have had this sheet of water in mind when writing in *The Passing of Arthur* of the King's command to Sir Bedivere:

> ". . . take Excalibur,
> And fling him far into the middle mere:
> Watch what thou seest, and lightly bring me word."

A similar claim is made for Dozmary Pool on Bodmin Moor.

The path, or drive, skirts the Pool (the house is seen on the right), and by keeping the Pool on the left we presently leave by the lodge gates and drop down to the sands at **Loe Bar.** This bar divides the sea from the Pool. The legendary story of its formation is that the wicked Tregeagle, carrying a sack of sand, was pursued by the Devil, and in his agitation carelessly dropped his burden in the very entry to the Pool. Occasionally the Pool would overflow its banks and cause trouble at Helston, so the bar was cut, after solemn petition to the lord of the manor, to give the waters egress to the sea. Now the height of water is regulated by culverts. The Bar is not pleasant walking, but it is of interest because on the Pool side are sometimes found extremely rare plants, such as the Strapwort.

From the Bar there is a good view of Porthleven and the spacious **Mount's Bay,** on the farther side of which are Penzance and Newlyn, described in our companion *Red Guide to West Cornwall.* Before us the mighty black cliffs predict stiff climbing.

About 2 miles from Loe Bar is **Baulk Head.** The lofty point which is seen to extend seaward for some distance is **Halzaphron Cliff,** noteworthy as the last spot on our shores where the bodies of shipwrecked folk were given unconsecrated burial. Apart from the fine view across to Mount's Bay, there is no special inducement to walk to its extremity, so the nearer road may be taken directly down to—

Church Cove, Gunwalloe,

which offers ample material to writers of romance and adventure with a substratum of fact.

(*a*) A notorious buccaneer, Captain Emery, is reputed to have buried a vast treasure, in chests, in the sandbanks close to the church. In 1770, one John Knill, Collector of Customs at St. Ives, procured a grant of treasure-trove, but his extensive operations were fruitless.

(*b*) In 1785 a vessel was wrecked here. A portion of the cargo comprised 2½ tons of money, and for many years subsequently each successive storm washed coins on to the beach. In 1845 a determined effort was made to sink a dollar mine. A dam was to be constructed, the water pumped out, and the dollars comfortably brought to the surface. A breeze from the south-west quickly removed all traces of the labour of many weeks, and later attempts have been similarly defeated.

Gunwalloe Church—at one time surrounded by the village but which has now been rebuilt farther inland—romantically situated and sheltered behind a cliff, has a square detached tower, 14 feet distant, built right into the rock which forms part of its north sides. The church is so close to the sea that the spray dashes over it in times of storm. The interior contains much of interest, notably some of the woodwork, new and old. The north aisle is fourteenth-century. Note the font (recently restored) and the roofs of the south porch and south aisle. St. Winwaloëi is the patron saint here, as at the Lizard.

The little headland behind Gunwalloe Church tower is called the **Castle Mound.** This was a prehistoric cliff fortress but little remains of the original earthwork. The separate church tower is no part of it but is similar to that found in many Cornish churches. Inland are the excellent links of the *Mullion Golf Club* (*see* p. 68). *Motorists* should bear in mind that a stream and loose sand make the coast impassable at Gunwalloe. *See* pp. 18–19.

A mile and a half inland from Gunwalloe is **Cury.** The ancient Church of St. Corantyn shows early features. The Norman south door; the ancient cross, 9 feet high, with wheel head; the hagioscope, and rood-loft stairways are interesting.

The ancient family seat of *Bonython*, in this parish, is of interest because from a member of the family, Captain Richard Bonython, one of the first emigrants to America, the poet Longfellow was descended. The captain settled at Saco, where he died in 1650.

From Gunwalloe the cliff-path rises steeply and as steeply falls to—

Poldhu Cove,

overlooked by the large hotel. Poldhu became world-famous as the site of the Marconi Wireless Telegraphy Station from which the first experimental trans-Atlantic morse signals were sent and received. It was from this station, too, that successful tests were made between Poldhu and Sydney on a wavelength of 100 metres and a power of about 30 kilowatts—tests which did much to direct attention to the possibilities of short-wave "beam" wireless. The station has been dismantled, but a monument recalls the association of the place with Marconi.

At Poldhu the stream is crossed by a stone bridge, and the road in less than 2 miles brings one to Mullion. The cliff path passes the *Poldhu Hotel* above the Cove, on Poldhu Point, and then descends into a narrow valley, with a number of bungalows; beyond is Polurrian Cove with a pleasant beach.

Beyond Polurrian the whitewashed stones must be carefully followed, and shortly **Mullion Cove,** amid the choicest Lizard scenery, lies before us.

Mullion

Approach.—By Western Region railway to Camborne. Thence by bus to Mullion, *via* Cury and Golf Links. By motor from the principal centres in Cornwall.
Distances from Mullion.—By cliff-path to Loe Bar, 4½ miles; Porthleven, 6 miles, Kynance, 6 miles. By road to Helston (*via* Penhale), 8 miles; Coverack 10 miles; Lizard Town and Head, 6 miles.

Road Routes.—*See* Motoring section.

Hotels.—*Mullion Cove; Polurrian; Old Inn; Gweal-an-Drea; Poldhu.*

Golf Links.—(18 holes). A beautifully situated sporting course on sandy turf by the sea.

Except perhaps for Lizard Town, Mullion is the most considerable village on the Lizard. There are shops and banks, some furnished cottages and bungalows and a number of boarding-houses and hotels.

Mullion village which is about a mile inland from the Cove, has many natural attractions and grand walks abound. The large modern hotels are on the cliffs.

The square-towered **Church** (Sundays 8, 11, 6), dedicated to St. Melan, was rebuilt in 1500, but there are remains of thirteenth-century work in chancel and tower. The bench-ends are extremely fine, and there is a good modern chancel screen. Note the original south door and latchet, supposed to have been inserted to facilitate the ejection of intruding dogs. The font is fifteenth-century. The registers date from 1598. In the churchyard (as at Helston Parish Church), the names of some of the departed are inscribed in unusually large letters.

The air of Mullion is mild yet bracing, and it is a noteworthy fact that Mullion is looked upon by many people as a kind of sanatorium.

At **Angrouse**, near Mullion, several barrows have been opened, disclosing interesting prehistoric remains. The fragments of an urn, some calcined bones and a bronze dagger found here are in the Truro Museum.

From the village a good road runs down beside the combe ending in —

Mullion Cove

Car Park on way down to Cove. **Road Routes.**—*See* Motoring section.

The Cove, with its miniature Harbour, is about a mile distant from the village. This is a delightful spot at whatever state of tide it is visited, though it should be seen at least twice —at low tide and at high tide in a south-westerly wind, when the waves hurl themselves against the harbour wall and throw up immense clouds of spray. The scenery contrasts strongly with that at Kynance only a few miles south. Above rise on all sides hoary, lichen-covered cliffs, rocks piled on rocks, vaulted, tunnelled, ribbed and groined, with chasms and natural arches, like the ruins of some vast cathedral. At low tide a good stretch of sand affords safe and enjoyable bathing. On a fine day the view seawards, with **Mullion Island** across the blue water, is one of imposing grandeur, yet clothed with a soft beauty that fires the imagination of the poet and inspires the artist. The island is about a mile in circumference and has at half-tide a remarkable similarity to a lion *couchant*. The **Gull Rock,** the home of countless sea birds, is also conspicuous. There are two caves, which can be explored at low water; by far the finer is that from which the Island is not visible, but dead low water is necessary for a visit. Teas and refreshments may be obtained at the Cove.

Mullion to Lizard Town by the Coast

This walk includes the cream of the Lizard coast scenery. The distance on the map is about 6 miles, but in view of the succession of steep hills few walkers will make the journey in less than 2½ to 3 hours. The best way is to allow as much of a whole day as remains after the journeys to Mullion and from the Lizard have been made.

From Mullion Cove the path climbs steeply, with precipitous

cliffs on the right, and over a majestic deep blue or dark green sea calling for constant admiration, is a magnificent panorama of Mount's Bay.

At **Pradanack Head** (256 ft.), the serpentine rock is noticeable. Several coves follow in succession, with sandy strips at the bottom of the black rocks, and bright yellow lichen covering the heights. *Frequent cliff falls make it unwise to venture too near the cliff edge.*

Vellan Head is next reached, and then amid impressive scenery we descend into **Gue Graze,** noted for its soapstone. The special quality of this rock was discovered by R. Chaffers, in 1755, and it was largely used in the manufacture of porcelain. Wedgwood acknowledged that in Chaffers and his material he had a serious rival. In 1775 a lease of the soaprock was bought by the Worcester Porcelain Company. The clay was worth about £20 a ton. The disused quarry will be seen on the right.

The scenery here is grand and awe-inspiring. Beyond Gue Graze is **Pigeon Ogo,** or Hugo, a fearful little cove with perpendicular cliffs 200 feet high. Beyond is the **Horse,** which juts some distance seawards. There is a cave here. From **Rill Head,** the next promontory, we look across to the Lizard, and a long winding path brings us down to far-famed Kynance.

Kynance Cove

Access.—About half a mile north of Lizard Town, a rough lane leaves the main road. It rapidly deteriorates to a mere track (unsuitable for cars, even in dry weather), but no difficulty will be found in following it westward to the coast. In about three-quarters of a mile the opening of the Cove is seen ahead, and one looks for the zigzag track leading down to the valley and the Cove itself. There are several other routes for walkers, the main point being to take a north-westerly course from Lizard Town.

Less than a mile north of Lizard Town, along the main Helston Road (A3083), is a Toll road which in 1¼ miles leads to the extensive Car Park and Kynance Cliff Hotel and Tea-Rooms within a few hundred yards of the top of the Cove. The toll charge includes car park *fee*.

Viewed at any state of the tide, either from the cliffs above or from the path leading down to the Cove, Kynance is entrancing. But, to appreciate its awe-inspiring grandeur, its rock formation, and its colouring to the full, it is essential to descend to the firm sandy beach at low tide. The way is unmistakable, the path not very steep nor particularly "heady" and there are easier ways for those inclined to dizziness. Most of the beach is uncovered for nearly five hours at a time (roughly 2½ hours before and 2½ hours after low water), twice every 24 hours 51 mins, in normal conditions. Before visiting Kynance readers are advised to inquire time of low tide on the day of their proposed visit and to arrange to arrive 2½ hours earlier.

It is quite impossible to describe the beauty of Kynance. Every visitor receives different impressions, but all will agree with Lord Leighton, who described it as "perfectly unique; a lovely picture, the finest cove in the kingdom."

Kynance is one of the most popular spots for a bathe on the whole Cornish coast, and on a fine day every cave and cranny and every scrap of "cover" is utilized to the full (and even beyond) to provide dressing accommodation. *It is unwise to bathe at low water.*

There are so many items of interest in this delicious spot that it is hard to know where to begin. The view seawards is divided by **Asparagus Island,** connected with the mainland at low water by a beach of the palest and finest sand imaginable.

Immediately south of Asparagus Island and separated from it by a narrowing channel is the lengthy **Gull Rock,** often thought to be part of the island.

Midway between the rocks and Asparagus Island rises, with perpendicular sides, the huge **Steeple Rock,** so prominent a feature of Kynance views. From the sands, the charming double view of the sea, with the wonderful colours of the rocks themselves, make one realize that there is no other place quite like Kynance.

For the caves, turn to the right. The first is termed the **Kitchen,** but no sanded kitchen floor ever approached this for whiteness. We can now closely examine the wonderful serpentine rock, for Kynance is entirely composed of this brilliant-hued stone. Of course, the surface is rougher when polished by the ocean than by hand or machinery, but many prefer it in this state. Nevertheless the surface is often polished enough to be slippery and care needs to be exercised in climbing or stepping on it.

The next cave is the **Parlour,** with a superb "bay" window. By a slight scramble over the rocks we reach the **Ladies' Bathing Pool**—small, sequestered, and perfectly safe at all states of the tide. Crossing the sands to Asparagus Island (passing the Sugar Loaf and Steeple) we mount the rocks a little way to inspect a wonderful sport of nature, the **Devil's Letter Box** and **Bellows.** At certain states of the tide, and owing to crevices under Asparagus Island, the water is forced with stupendous power through a small vent, accompanied by a roar like the discharge of artillery, and a heavy shower of spray.

Returning to the sands, the **Drawing-Room** is close at hand, composed of beautiful green serpentine. On either side of the **Bishop's Rock** the outline of a face is easily discernible. High above Bishop's Rock will be noticed a great cavity called the **Devil's Mouth.**

Even those unable to walk all the way from Mullion to the Lizard should find time for that onward from Kynance. **Tor Balk,** the first cliff to be surmounted, rewards us with enchanting views of the delicious cove. Next comes **Yellow Carn Head,** with the **Lion Rock** below. Eighty acres of Lizard Downs including the eastern side of Kynance Cove are in the care of the National Trust.

From Pentreath Beach, beyond Yellow Carn, a rough lane leads to Lizard Town, but it is well worth while to keep to the increasingly rugged coast.

Lizard Town

Road Routes, *see* Motoring section.
Car Parks in several places, many free.

Lizard Town is a medium-sized straggling and somewhat plain village having a few good hotels and a number of boarding-houses. Almost every other cottage or hut is a miniature "Serpentine Works" where the far-famed and beautifully coloured and mottled serpentine rock is cut, polished and made into many useful and ornamental articles, including: ashtrays, necklaces, serviette-rings, model lighthouses, candle-sticks, clock cases and lamp standards. The "town" is half a mile inland from Lizard Head, east of which is the site of—

The Lizard Lighthouse

Admission.—Visitors are conducted over the building on weekdays between 1 p.m. and an hour before sunset, *except when the fog sirens are in action.*

A visit to this famous lighthouse is of more than usual interest, on account of the deadly nature of the headland and its unique position on the most southerly spot in England. The officials who conduct visitors round will explain the working of the machinery. The lighthouse was erected in 1752, but altered in 1903. There were formerly what are known as "twin lights," one at either end of the buildings, each with fixed white lights. A white flashing electric light of 4 million candle-power, one of the most powerful in the world, is now projected from the eastern tower only.

Immediately west of the southernmost point is **Polpeor Cove,** for many years a station of the Lifeboat service, but now removed to Kilcobben. To the west of Polpeor Cove is Pistil Hogo where in the meadow at the back it is reputed that after a shipwreck 200 bodies were buried.

Off the point just east of the lighthouse is an isolated rock called the *Bumble*. Its base can be reached at low water. The inlet to the east of it is **Housel Bay,** protected on its far side by Penolver Point, a grandly piled rocky headland on which the former *Lloyds Signal Station* is conspicuous. The bay has a popular bathing beach and is only about eight minutes' walk from Lizard Town. But before striking inland, one should not miss taking a look at the **Lion's Den,** a great pit in the cliff just east of the Lighthouse, formed by the collapse of the roof of the innermost portion of a cavern. By the continued action of the sea through the entrance of the cave, the portion of the superstructure which fell in has been washed out. The result is the formation of a huge funnel, piercing the cliff vertically, and having an entrance from the sea. It is best seen at high tide with a south-easterly wind. The Den is similar to the Frying Pan, near Cadgwith, a few miles round the east coast of the Lizard.

Landewednack Church. About half a mile east of Lizard Town, this is the most southerly church in England. It is pleasantly situated in a tree-lined valley which—barely a mile from bleak Lizard Town—invariably astonishes visitors. As a matter of fact, however, the east coast of the promontory can offer many similar surprises. The Lizard is in Landewednack parish. The church is dedicated to St. Wynwallow. A late Norman doorway surrounds a Perpendicular doorway. At the angle of the south chapel and chancel is a hagioscope. The font dates from 1414, and bears the inscription "Ric. Bolham Me Fecit." The stone-groined porch dates from 1300. In the church hangs, as in several other Cornish churches, a copy of the address issued by Charles I from Sudeley Camp to his "brave Cornish subjects."

Church Cove is reached by a pretty but narrow lane from the church. The lane suddenly becomes a rough path, dropping rapidly to the Cove. Just before the Cove a cliff path to the south ascends to above **Kilcobben Cove** where is a new Lifeboat Station superseding the former stations of the Lizard and Cadgwith. There is a flight of 160 steps down to the lifeboat house (the lift is not for public use). The "Duke of Cornwall" is one of the most modern and best equipped lifeboats in the service.

THE EAST COAST OF THE LIZARD,

though less renowned than the west, can be recommended to walkers who like to get off the beaten track, for with the exception of Cadgwith and Coverack there are no rivals to the popularity of Kynance and Mullion, and one can tramp for miles without meeting anyone.

Starting from Church Cove we mount **The Balk,** with its tall day-mark. In Polbarrow Bay is an old disused pilchard "cellar." **Carnbarrow** is a fine natural archway. **Ravens Hugo** and **Dollar Hugo** are grand caves (serpentine), and should be visited by boat from Cadgwith. Just before reaching Cadgwith, and where the path turns off to the left, is the **Devil's Frying Pan.** This, too, should be inspected by boat from Cadgwith. Formerly it was a cave, but, as happened at the Lion's Den (p. 73), the roof fell in, and the constant washing of the sea has resulted in a curious cliff formation.

Cadgwith

Although one of the lesser known Cornish coves by reason of its comparative inaccessibility, Cadgwith Cove is one of the most picturesque to be found anywhere in the Duchy. The approach, after leaving Ruan Minor, is down a winding, very steep and narrow lane which brings the visitor quite suddenly to the miniature cove, with its thatched-roofed, stone-built cottages. The two small beaches are separated by "The Todden," a diminutive headland leading to a secluded natural bathing pool amongst the rocks.

Cadgwith (*Cadgwith Hotel*) lies at the mouth of a pretty, well-wooded valley and is a small and very compact little village tucked neatly between high, rocky headlands and completely unspoiled by the march of time. The local fishermen do a thriving business in crabs and lobsters.

With grand opportunities for fishing, bathing and walking, Cadgwith is an ideal spot for those in search of a restful holiday amid quiet, peaceful and very beautiful surroundings. Accommodation is limited and inquiries should be made a long time in advance.

Two miles inland is **Ruan Major,** the pinnacled tower of its church (now closed) peering over the tree-tops a short way east of the busy main road. It is of little interest.

Ruan Minor, from which the narrow, winding lane descends to Cadgwith, is a passably pretty village. The little church was formerly smaller still, for the north aisle and creeper-covered tower were added in the fifteenth century. It contains a Norman font. The registers date from 1653.

Leaving Cadgwith with regret, we pass the coast-watchers' look-out and **Kildown Point,** and so on to **Ynys Head.** Another ½ mile brings us to that charming spot, **Poltesco.** This rocky gorge (it is hardly a valley) is picturesque in the extreme. The hills are steep and fairly well covered. Huge boulders divert the stream into cascades as it flows to the sea at **Carleon Cove.** Formerly Poltesco was famed for its serpentine quarries and works; the old buildings and waterwheel remain. (Motorists should beware of the dangerously steep direct road from Ruan Minor.)

From Poltesco there is a beautiful cliff path to the pleasantly situated **Kennack Sands,** (car park, caravan sites) a quiet and peaceful spot amid rural surroundings, which offers tempting opportunities for bathing. By following up the streams the botanist may find many treasures. The road down to the Sands leaves the road over Goonhilly Downs from Traboe Cross at **Kuggar** where is the last shop you will see till you come to Coverack.

A walk of 2½ miles along bold cliffs brings us to Black Head, passing two headlands, off which are set the rocky groups of **Carrick Luz** and **Pedn Boar.** It is a stiff climb up to **Black Head** (230 ft. high), the most important promontory between the Lizard and Falmouth and a fine viewpoint.

In another mile we pass **Porthbeer Cove** and **Chynhalls Point**—the path going behind the hotel—and drop down by way of **Perprean Cove** to the quaint and picturesque village of—

Coverack

This is a typical Cornish fishing village, complete with stone-built whitewashed cottages, a miniature harbour and a life-boat station. In recent years a modern settlement has attached itself but, so far, this has not detracted from the picturesqueness of the old village. There are hotels and guest-houses available, for an increasing number of people are visiting this charming little place (*Headland; Paris; Bay; Channel View*). Fishing for bass and pollack is a favourite pastime.

Coverack had a great reputation years ago for its "free" traffic. The first coastguard officer in his first annual report stated that in the preceding twelve months, in spite of the utmost vigilance, no fewer than 7,000 ankers of brandy had been successfully "run" ashore in the bay. He naturally asked for more men. Coverack and Mullion boasted the greatest number of smuggling successes.

The cliff path northward from the village has been much improved but **Lowland Point** (*National Trust*) is best approached from St. Keverne by footpaths via Trevean or Trebarveth Farms.

The Manacles. Off St. Keverne is the particularly dangerous reef called The Manacles—*Maen-eglos*—church stones. St. Keverne Church, on the high ground above, is a well-known mariner's mark. One rock, covered at high water, stands about a mile and a half from the shore. Here occurred the disaster to the *Mohegan* in October 1898, when over a hundred lives were lost. A memorial in the churchyard recalls the event. A few months later the liner *City of Paris* went aground at the nearby lowlands, but fortunately without loss of life. The Manacle Rocks provide the best fishing ground between Falmouth and the Lizard.

Porthoustock, entered by a steep hill, is a tiny fishing village, situated in a cove between steep hills. There is no inn. Vessels call here and ship stone from the St. Keverne quarry works, which scar the cliffs on either side of the cove. Much of this material is in the form of "chippings" and "fine granite" for reinforced concrete piles and works. A good deal of "road metal" is also shipped from here.

A pleasant walk through the fields and woods by a path on the right of the cove leads to—

St. Keverne

Hotels.—*White Hart; Three Tuns Inn.*
Telegraph and Post Office.

Distance.—Eleven miles from Helston; 1¾ miles from the Manacle Rocks.

This is an interesting village which forms a good headquarters for those exploring the eastern coast of the Lizard; to the north the scenery is wooded and very undulating; to the west lie the vast heathery expanses of Goonhilly with the great G.P.O. satellite tracking station.

The fine old **Church,** which was re-dedicated to St. Keverne in 1266, has undergone many alterations. There are three sets of rood stairs, indicating that the building was extended eastward at least twice. The tower, 60 feet high, is surmounted by a spire of 38 feet, and is a familiar landmark to passing vessels on account of its proximity to the dreaded Manacles. The bench-ends are well worth careful examination. In the south-west corner is a curiosity in "The Gudgeon from H.M. Brig o' War *Primrose*," lost on the Manacles in 1809. From the churchyard there is a magnificent view over Falmouth Bay.

In this parish is a dolmen or cromlech of great interest to antiquaries called *The Three Brothers of Grugith.* The stones are fully described in *Nænia Cornubiæ*, they represent a Bronze Age burial stone cist, the largest in Cornwall.

In connection with the three stones a legend is related which, if true, throws a lurid light on the not infallible character of a saint. St. Just was preparing to leave the habitation of his friend St. Keverne, after a convivial evening, when he was seized with the lust of desire for mundane things. Possibly their libations of well-water were heavy—even for saints. Anyway, he coveted the chalice of his host, and artfully suggested, after repeated and copious draughts, that St. Keverne should proceed to the well to refill the stoup for a final drink. When St. Keverne returned with the liquor, both St. Just and the chalice had vanished. St. Keverne pursued and picked up three stones for missiles. Overtaking St. Just near the Helston road, he threw the stones at him, and the guilty saint dropped the chalice. Hence the Stones, or "Brothers," of Grugith.

From Porthoustock the coast path leads to **Porthallow** (*Five Pilchards Inn*). This is a very pleasantly situated, unspoiled fishing village, backed by steep, wooded hills and complete with a wide beach. From the beach there are grand views beyond Nare Head (on left) over Falmouth Bay.

Bold **Nare Point,** not to be confused with Nare Head, lies just over a mile to the north. In passing we enjoy a lovely view across the mouth of Helford River, with Rosemullion Head beyond, and Mawnan Church perched high in the cliffs. Right across Falmouth Bay, to the north-eastward, rise Pendennis Head and Zoze Point, guarding the entrance to Falmouth Harbour. In another ⅓-mile we are abreast of **Gillan Creek.** There is no ferry from Gillan but during the summer a boat from St. Anthony may pull across, and so save a mile or two. If no boat is obtainable proceed by way of Carne, at the head of the Creek. Past the mill leads one to the hamlet of—

St. Anthony-in-Meneage

It would be hard to conceive a greater contrast to the stern, relentless Lizard cliffs than this sweet spot, hidden among trees at the extremity of Dennis Head. St. Anthony Church, according to tradition, was erected as a votive offering, soon after the Conquest, by certain Normans of rank, who were storm-driven against the Cornish coast. The ship brought its living freight in safety to Gillan Creek. The church contains an Early English window in chancel, and Perpendicular architecture, but there are no Norman remains. The thirteenth-century inscribed font is interesting, and there is a holy-water stoup of the same period.

The view from **Dennis Head** is unusually grand. The promontory was fortified during the Civil War to protect Helford shipping. *Kingdom's Weekly Intelligence* thus recorded the fall of the garrison: "March 17, 1646. S. Dennis Fort, at Helford, with 26 pieces of ordnance, is surrendered. It is a place of consequence, and will conduce much to the blocking up Pendennis Castle."

The extensive grounds and plantations of *Bosahan* (pronounced *Bow-sane*) now make it necessary to leave the cliff. The best route to follow is the charming riverside road from St. Anthony to Manaccan, whence it is a mile to Helford village by a road that finally winds down through woods.

Manaccan

Inn.—*New Inn.*
Telegraph and Post Office.

Distances.—Ten miles from Helston; One mile from Helford.

Manaccan is one of the five parishes comprising the Meneage —"Land of Monks." It overlooks the head of the Gillan creek amid charming scenery, and forms the goal of a very popular boat trip from Falmouth. The village stands on a hill, the houses being built irregularly round the church, sloping sharply downhill. Here begins a valley walk beside the *Durra*, a stream of surpassing loveliness.

The dedication of the fine old *Church*, the earliest part of which dates from the twelfth century, is uncertain. It has been ascribed to a St. Manaccus (the window in the transept), but it is doubtful whether a saint of that name existed. *Manaccus* in the Cornish language meant *The Monk*, and it is probable that the church was built near the site of the cell of an old Celtic monk or hermit. The church is known throughout Cornwall on account of the ancient fig-tree growing out of the south wall near the tower. It has been *in situ* for at least two hundred years. The church was restored *c.* 1890. The roof is an exact copy of the original, though less finely carved; parts of the old roof were used in the pulpit, the altar rails, and the two fine chairs at the east end. The rood stairs were opened up about 1930 but no trace of the rood itself remains.

Manaccan has an interesting connection with Captain Bligh (Bligh of the *Bounty*). While surveying for the Admiralty in the Helford River during the Napoleonic Wars, he was arrested by the local constable as a French spy, and brought to the magistrate, who was Richard Polwhele, Vicar of Manaccan. Polwhele was at tea, and ordered the prisoner to be put in the lock-up—later the vicarage coal cellar. When sent for, Bligh refused to say a word unless all but himself and the vicar were excluded. He then disclosed his name and business. Polwhele records that they spent the night in great friendliness, and he corresponded with Bligh for years afterwards.

Helford

Helford village, which straddles the creek, is an idyllic spot in a beautifully-wooded combe. The road continues round the creek to the right and ends at the *Shipwright's Arms*. At all times, Helford is very beautiful, but it is at its best at high water any June morning, when every other cottage is bedecked with roses of varying shades. A **Pedestrian Ferry** runs on request daily (*Easter to October, 15p.*) to the *Ferry Boat Inn* at **Helford Passage** across the estuary, from whence it is but six miles from **Trebah,** at top of hill, to Falmouth (bus service).

Helford River

This is the large estuary midway between Falmouth and the Lizard. Were it not for the bar which regulates the entry and exit of vessels drawing more than a few feet of water, this delightful river would be even more visited. The scenery is beautiful—like that of the Fal, though on smaller scale.

During summer pleasure craft of all descriptions utilise

Helford waters for anchorage. The **Duchy of Cornwall Oyster Farm,** the property of the Duke of Cornwall, is carried on in this river, the headquarters being at **Port Navas,** set at the head of a little creek amidst a scene of sylvan beauty. It is one of the finest oyster farms in Great Britain. The fishery is now leased to Mac Fisheries, Ltd.

The river is tidal up to **Gweek** (*Gweek Inn*), on the Long Downs—Dodson's Gap road to the Lizard. Today there is a quiet little harbour at Gweek and coal is discharged, but in the fourteenth century this was the port of Helston.

Many visitors express surprise on discovering that the beauty of the Lizard promontory is not confined to its rugged coastline. Reference has already been made to the extensive moorland known as Goonhilly Downs; a further variety of scene is presented to those who explore the corner bounded by the Gweek-St. Keverne road, for here heathery downs give way to sheltered combes, well wooded and watered. Through such scenes passes the road from Manaccan to Gweek, *via*—

Mawgan

(Distances.—From Helston, 5 miles; from Gweek, 2 miles),

or **Mawgan-in-Meneage** as it is styled to distinguish it from other Mawgans. The thirteenth-century Church which was enlarged in the fifteenth century is mainly Perpendicular, but the south transept and chancel are Decorated. On the north side are rood-loft stairs. There are some interesting objects within, notably the cross-legged stone effigy of a knight and a lady. The knight is conjectured to be Roger Carminow, who was in Palestine with Edward I. There are also several monuments to the Vyvyans of Trelowarren. The tower is considered the finest in West Cornwall. There are some quaint lines on a brass to Haniball Basset, each line containing the same words:

Shall wee all dye
wee shall dye all
all dye shall wee
dye all wee shall.

About five minutes' walk from the church, on a little green beside the Helston road, is **Mawgan Cross,** an inscribed stone, supposed to be a thousand years old.

Truro

Access.—*By road. See* Motoring section. Passenger Motor Launches from Falmouth according to tide.
Banks.—*Barclays* in King Street and Boscawen Street; *Lloyds, Midland, National Westminster,* in Boscawen Street; *Trustee Savings,* Princes Street.
Bowls.—At Kenwyn.
Buses.—Truro is an important centre, and buses run to and from Falmouth, Penzance, St. Agnes and Trevaunance Cove, Perranporth, Bodmin, Liskeard, and Okehampton, St. Austell, Redruth, Camborne, Portreath etc.
Car Parks.—The Green; Lemon Quay, at foot of Lemon Street; The Moorfield; Castle Street; Old Bridge Street.
Cattle Market.—Top of Castle Hill, Wednesday.
Cinema.—*Plaza,* Lemon Street.
Cricket.—Truro City Cricket Club, Boscawen Park.
Distances.—From London, 256 miles by road, 280 miles by rail. From Falmouth, 11 miles by road, 12 miles by rail, 9½ miles by water. From Penzance, 27 miles.
Early Closing Day.—Thursday.
Golf Links.—(18 holes.) Treliske, Redruth Road, about a mile from the town.
Hotels.—*Royal,* Lemon Street; *Brookdale,* Tregolls Road; *St. George's,* St. George's Road; *Carlton,* Falmouth Road; *Culroy,* Chapel Hall.
Library.—County Branch Library, Pydar Street.
Licensing Hours.—10.30–2.30 and 5.30–10.30. Sundays, 12–2 and 7–10.30.
Market Day.—Wednesday.
Museum and Art Gallery.—River Street. Admission free. Open April–Oct.: 10 a.m. to 5 p.m. Nov.–Mar., 10 a.m. to 4 p.m.
Places of Worship.—*The Cathedral, St. George's, St. Paul's. St. John's and Kenwyn;* Methodist—*St. Mary's, St. George's, St. Clement Street, City Mission and Lemon Chapel;* Baptist—*River Street;* Society of Friends—Truro Vean; Salvation Army—Kenwyn Street; Roman Catholic—*St. Piran and Our Lady of Portal,* St. Austell Street..
Population.—15,690.
Post Office.—G.P.O., High Cross—at west end of Cathedral. Sub-offices at St. Clement's Hill, Kenwyn Street, Malpas, Bodmin Road, Highertown, Daniell Street, Hendra Road.
Railway.—Western Region, Truro Station (Junction for Falmouth). Tel.: 0872–6244.
Tennis.—At Boscawen Park, beside the river, about a mile below the bridge.

Truro carries its age—nearly a thousand years—with ease. It is always clean, bright and busy, and has never been allowed to appear old, and when it assumed the dignity of a city in 1877 the title was in every way appropriate.

Truro holds a place of considerable importance in the Duchy, being the headquarters of Cornwall County Council and many other county and public bodies. It is the main shopping centre for the many rural districts around. Market Day sees Truro at its busiest for then buses and cars from outlying villages bring a constant stream of folk who come not only to shop, but also to meet their friends and relatives, and to exchange the latest gossip.

Boscawen Street and *Lemon Street* are the principal thoroughfares. In recent years many of the former solid looking Georgian buildings have given way to modern structures housing banks and supermarkets. The fine old building, the *Red Lion Hotel*, which faced up Lemon Street from Boscawen Street, was unfortunately demolished in 1967. *Samuel Foote* (1770–77) was born either here or in a house near by.

Truro is also a small port, and from *Worth's Quay* (approached by steps from Boscawen Bridge), motor launches make the beautiful trip down the Truro River, meeting the Fal about a mile and a half below Malpas, and continuing to Falmouth Town.

Near the quay is the *Western National Bus Centre*, with services to almost all parts of Cornwall. It is here, too, that the long-distance coaches stop to set down and pick up passengers on their way to and from London, the Midlands and Penzance. Near by, in Boscawen Street, is the very effective **War Memorial,** a bronze figure of a soldier on a pedestal of Cornish granite.

A stroll round Truro will reveal many unsuspected quaint and pleasant corners. There is a miniature stream, meandering along to join the Allen and Kenwyn rivers which, in turn, sidle along to swell the Truro River at the head of which the city stands.

At the top of Lemon Street is the imposing **Lander Memorial,** a Doric column erected to the memory of Richard and John Lander, who traced the river Niger to its exit to the sea in 1827.

With its excellent transport services Truro is a very convenient holiday centre, situated as it is within easy reach of Falmouth, St. Ives, Penzance, Fowey, etc. Nearer to hand are many pleasant walks including that along the river to Malpas (p. 87), passing **Boscawen Park** with its sub-tropical plants, shady seats, small lake and refreshment house. There are tennis, football and cricket grounds near by.

As the greater part of Truro lies in a bowl not many feet above sea-level, all exits are, perforce, uphill. A compensation is that, from the surrounding hills, excellent views are obtained right across the city with its stately three-spired Cathedral as

the focusing-point, and a lovely background of well-wooded and richly-coloured fields and pastures.

The Cathedral

Open to visitors on weekdays: June 24–Sept. 14, 7.15 a.m. to 7 p.m.; Sept. 15–30, 7.15 a.m. to 6 p.m.; Oct. 1–March 31, 7.15 a.m. to 5 p.m.; April 1– June 23, 7.15 a.m. to 6 p.m. On Sundays, Easter–Sept. 30, 7.30 a.m. to 12.30 p.m., 2 p.m. until close of Evensong. Oct. 1 to Easter, 7.30 a.m. to 12.30 p.m., 3 p.m. until close of Evensong. All parts are free and open.

Services.—Daily services (time liable to variation), 7.30, 7.45 a.m., and 4.15 p.m. Sunday services, 7.45, 8, 9.45, 11.15 and 6.15.

Dimensions.—Length from east to west, 300 feet; interior of the choir, 115 feet; nave, 165 feet. Width of nave, 76 feet. Width across transepts, 158 feet. Height of the interior, 70 feet.

Truro Cathedral may not have the age-worn beauty of its easterly neighbours at Exeter and Wells, but it is an extremely interesting building for those who know the older foundations by reason of the facts that it is one of the few cathedrals to have been built in modern times, and that it was raised by the united efforts of all religious denominations in a county which then was more inclined to non-conformity than to the Church.

J. L. Pearson, R.A., was the architect, and the style is Early English. The cloisters have still to be completed.

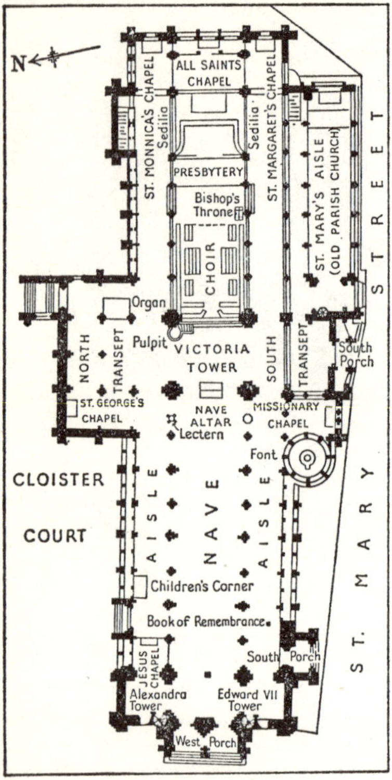

TRURO CATHEDRAL

King Edward VII (then Prince of Wales) laid the foundation stone in 1880, and the building was consecrated by the Archbishop of Canterbury in 1887. The benediction of the nave took place in 1903, in the presence of King George V and Queen Mary (then Prince and Princess of Wales), the Archbishop of Canterbury, and some thirty bishops.

The Central or **Victoria Tower,** 250 feet high, forms a Cornish Memorial to Queen Victoria. The western towers, 204 feet high, completed in 1909, are known as the **Edward VII** and **Alexandra Towers.**

Internally the light-grey stone of the building and the clear glass of the nave clerestory windows leave a rather bare effect which is, however, amply compensated by the fine proportions, the aisle windows and the richness of the reredos and east window. The Cathedral was raised on the site of the old Parish Church of St. Mary, the south aisle of which was retained to form the south aisle of the Cathedral, and here again the brightness of the nave provides a striking contrast. The aisle has the quiet charm of a beautiful old church of bygone generations. The old organ is here, and the pulpit deserves attention; so too does the carefully restored roof. West of the south transept is the **Baptistry**, a memorial to Henry Martyn, the great Truro missionary. It is an architectural gem, the stones and marbles forming a harmony of gorgeous tints.

The **Reredos**, of richly-carved Bath stone, is of great beauty. Behind it is the **Chapel of All Saints**, open daily for prayer and meditation.

In the north choir aisle the terra-cotta group by *Tinworth*, representing "Christ Going to Calvary", compels admiration by its beauty and dignity.

On the north wall of the North Transept is a monument to *John Robartes and his wife*, a fine specimen of the monumental art of the Jacobean period.

As a Jubilee gift, in 1935 the Freemasons of Cornwall presented the first bay of the **Cloisters**, opening out of the North Transept.

The Chapter House, dedicated in 1967, is a modern building of beauty and interest.

The Communion plate includes a gold chalice, paten and flagon richly chased. The Bishop's chalice is of gold and silver-gilt, ornamented with about three hundred gems given by various donors. There are two other chalices, three patens, a silver-gilt bread-dish, a silver-gilt flagon (the gift of Queen Alexandra), and a silver set.

Under the window—the most westerly on the south side—which contains the picture of John Wesley preaching at Gwennap Pit, is the *Book of Remembrance*, containing the names of some 4,000 Cornishmen who fell in the 1914–18 War.

The Royal Institution of Cornwall

(Admission free. April to October, 10 a.m. to 5 p.m. November to March 10 a.m. to 4 p.m.)

The Royal Institution of Cornwall was founded in 1818, and its **Museum and Art Gallery**, is well known. Many of the Cornish prehistoric objects exhibited are of exceptional interest and include ornaments and weapons of bronze and burial urns of "sun-baked" clay with typical ornamentation added while the clay was soft; also relics of the Stone Age. The Museum also contains an extensive collection of Cornish minerals; outstanding among these are specimens collected at the end of the eighteenth century during the boom years of Cornish mining by Philip Rashleigh; the "Davey" and "Tellam" collections illustrating the flora of Cornwall, and a well-mounted series of Cornish birds. Industrial Art is represented by the "De Pass" collection of furniture, pottery, porcelain, etc., and the "Hawkins" collection of Japanese lacquer and ivories. The "Bonython" gallery contains the fine art collection presented by A. A. de Pass and there are two Art Galleries containing works by many well-known artists. The Muniment Room contains several thousand manuscripts and documents and include those bequeathed to the Royal Institution by the Cornish historian, Charles Henderson, whose "Essays in Cornish History" should be studied by all interested in the history of the county.

Historical Note

In old records the city is variously called Treveru, Trieurew and Truruburgh. It is said that Truro was granted a charter of incorporation by Reginald FitzRoy, Earl of Cornwall, in 1140, which confirmed a charter previously granted by Richard de Lucy in 1135. Robert, Earl of Moreton, received the manor from the Conqueror, and it passed to Richard de Lucy, Chief Justiciary of England, in 1161.

From the time of King John, the Mayor had jurisdiction over the whole of Falmouth Harbour. Obviously, when Falmouth came into existence, and achieved such importance as a packet station, the port could no longer allow interference with its waters from a town a dozen miles away. (*See* p. 28.)

Truro was loyal during the Civil War. Here Sir Ralph Hopton made his headquarters in 1642, and again in 1646, prior to his surrender to Sir Thomas Fairfax. Prince Charles, afterwards Charles II, was entertained at Truro in the winter of 1645 and again in 1647.

The former Church of St. Mary, of which the south aisle is incorporated in the Cathedral, was built in the reign of Henry VIII. A deed is still preserved, dated the nineteenth year of the reign of King Henry VII (1504), by which Sir John Arundell gives permission for stone to be dug for the "byldynge of the new Church and of a new toure."

Truro was a coinage town by decree of King John; that is to say, the tin was brought here to be tested and stamped. Tin has been one of the principal factors in the city's wealth. The last of the Stannary Parliaments was held at Truro in 1752.

Queen Elizabeth granted Truro a charter of incorporation, with a mayor, four aldermen, and twenty burgesses. From the reign of Edward I until the redistribution of seats in 1885, Truro returned two members to Parliament.

THE NEIGHBOURHOOD OF TRURO

Truro is an excellent point from which to explore some of the little-visited villages and scenes cut off from the main tide of affairs by the ramifications of the creeks running into the Fal.

Tresillian, 3½ miles east of Truro, is situated at the point where the main road to St. Austell (bus services) crosses the head of **Tresillian Creek,** or river. The creek joins the Truro river at Malpas, about 3 miles away, wandering amid thickly-wooded hills. Remains of earthworks on neighbouring estates give evidence of many combats in the district. At Tresillian Bridge, in 1646, the treaty of peace was declared between Sir Ralph Hopton and Sir Thomas Fairfax by which the former's regiment of horse was to be disbanded and Truro quietly surrendered to Cromwell's representatives.

A pretty return walk to Truro can be made *via* Pencalenick and St. Clement. At the turn in the road a mile from Tresillian

Bridge cross a stile on the left, beside a wood, then over the Pencalenick Ponds by the narrow causeway and by the road bordering the Tresillian river to—

St. Clement

The village, 1½ miles south-east of Truro, is prettily situated on the banks of the Tresillian river.

The thirteenth-century *Church* is deserving of note. In 1849 several ancient mural paintings were discovered, representing the Crucifixion, the Triumphal Entry into Jerusalem, the Flight into Egypt, etc. The ancient font was discovered in a ditch, where it had lain for more than half a century. In 1865 the building was subjected to one of those "renovations" which should be called "spoliation," for the old roof, benches and nearly everything of interest were swept away, including the paintings mentioned above. Recently the interior furnishings have been re-arranged in accord with modern ideas of worship.

Near the porch is the famous Ignioc Stone which has been a national monument since 1932. The rude inscription, IGNIOC VITAL FILI TORRICI, is read, "Igniocus Vitalis son of Torricus." This is, regarded as the finest of Cornwall's inscribed stones. It dates from the third century.

From St. Clement it is only a mile by field-path to—

Malpas

(*Heron Hotel*), a very ancient little port. The place itself is of no interest, but the views towards the Fal, and along the Truro and Tresillian rivers are enchanting. Passengers from Falmouth land at Malpas when the tide does not serve for Truro.

Leland records a desperate fight near Malpas. A French ship-of-war was chased by eighteen Spanish merchant ships into Falmouth Harbour. The Frenchman endeavoured to escape up the Fal, but was brought to bay off Malpas. The fight was most severe. A cannon-ball 3½ inches in diameter, picked up a few years since in a neighbouring wood, was possibly a stray shot from this encounter.

Across the water from Malpas is **Woodbury,** where lived Henry Martyn, the martyr missionary, whose memorial is in Truro Cathedral. Woodbury is a noted spot for river picnics.

Kea is 2 miles south-west of Truro, in a luxuriant part of the county once busy with mining. **Coombe,** nearly 3 miles south of Truro and on the east side of the Falmouth road, is very prettily situated in a small creek off the Fal, half a mile north-west of King Harry Passage. It is noted for its plum gardens.

In the churchyard of the village of **Baldhu,** 4½ miles to the west, lies the body of Billy Bray, the celebrated Cornish Methodist preacher. His famous "Three-Eyed" Chapel is still to be seen half a mile farther north-west of the church, on the road leading to Chacewater.

Feock, 5 miles south of Truro, is charmingly situated, with Restronguet Creek on one side and the broad Carrick Roads on the other. The church has a tower and belfry separated from the main building, as is sometimes seen elsewhere in Cornwall. Above the curious old lych gate, and forming part of it, is a small "parish room." The only other similar lych gates in the county are at Wendron (3 miles north of Helston), and at Kenwyn (Truro) and St. Clement.

Devoran (*Devoran Inn*), some 4½ miles south-west of Truro, has access to the sea by Restronguet Creek, and the export of minerals and the import of coals, etc., for the mines in the Gwennap district formerly brought brisk trade to the Quay. A good road leads pleasantly to Penpoll and Feock.

St. Michael Penkevil is 3½ miles south-east of Truro *via* Malpas Ferry. The church, dating from 1261, was restored by G. E. Street in 1862–6, and contains several monuments to the Boscawens (Viscounts Falmouth).

Tregothnan, the magnificent seat of Viscount Falmouth, stands in this parish, on high ground overlooking King Harry's Reach. It was built, in Tudor style, in 1818, by Edward Boscawen, 4th Viscount and 1st Earl of Falmouth.

Lamorran is a little place near the western bank of the river Fal. The tiny thirteenth-century church of St. Moran was rebuilt in 1853. The registers date from 1573. **Lamorran Creek,** on the Fal, has some charming scenery.

Ruan Lanihorne

(*King's Head Inn*) is at the head of the navigable portion of the Fal. The fine old Church of St. Rumon contains Norman remains. In 1866 an effigy was discovered in a thirteenth-century arch. This was supposed to be the shrine of St. Rumon, but authorities discredit the tradition. In the neighbourhood is a remarkable instance of the changes wrought in a district by the blocking-up of a river. Years ago the Fal, a deep river, penetrated 4 miles beyond Ruan Lanihorne. It was navigable indeed as far as—

Tregony

(*Town Arms Hotel*), a borough from the time of James I until 1832. Without doubt Tregony was a thriving, busy town on the banks of the Fal, long before Penryn and Truro. There is evidence that the tide ebbed and flowed at Tregony Quay. From very early times Tregony had the right of sending two burgesses to Parliament. The ancient tin mines and later, the china clay pits were the ruin of the place, for the Fal brought down sand and rubbish from them in such quantities that the bed of the river was choked. Two Acts of Parliament, passed by Henry VIII, failed to stop the tin mining. Little by Little the waters shrank from the old town, until now, there is little more than a stream a few feet wide at this point and the navigable portion is more than 4 miles distant. Consequently, Tregony, situated on the slope of a steep hill, has now become a sleepy village.

In 1761 some miners made a remarkable discovery when working in ground which had formed part of the burial place of the defunct church of St. James. A coffin was discovered 11 feet 3 inches long, and 3 feet 9 inches deep, containing a gigantic skeleton. The remains crumbled to dust on the admission of air. A tooth, however, which remained entire, measured, it is said, 2½ inches in length. Evidently the Cornish giants had a real and substantial existence.

The ancient town (now little more than a village) of **Grampound,** on the main stream of the Fal, like its sister Tregony, once enjoyed commercial prosperity and Parliamentary representation. The pier of an early bridge (the "Grand Pont" which gave the place its name) that once spanned the river can no longer be seen. Here, as at Tregony, it will be noticed that refuse from the China-clay workings farther north gives the Fal a milky-white appearance. Among many old houses the most notable is the ancient manor house, the ceilings of which are famous. In the small market place is a very old but mutilated Cornish monument, originally a kind of cross.

Between Grampound and Truro is **Probus.** The *Church of SS. Probus and Grace* was made collegiate by King Athelstan, A.D. 926. The richly-carved tower, 125 feet 10 inches high and the highest in Cornwall, is considered by many the finest in the county. It dates from the time of Henry VIII. There are some fine houses in the neighbourhood, notably **Trewithen** with its fine garden (*Garden only: weekday afternoons from March to June and in September; House and Garden: open Thursdays* 2–4.30 *May–September. Charge*).

St. Austell and Mevagissey

The busy town of St. Austell is the gateway to a district which is very popular with holiday-makers. The great attraction is the number of coves and bays, all of them safe and sandy and ideal for children. One or two of these are close to a village, but many visitors stay at a farm a short way inland, and with the aid of a car visit various beaches in turn, according to wind, tide and other conditions. The western edge of the district, along by Portholland and Portloe, has already been described.

ST. AUSTELL

Access.—*Rail.*—St. Austell station is on the Western Region main line, and most trains stop. Tel: St. Austell 3452.
Road Routes.—See pp. 11–15.
Banks.—*Barclays, Lloyds, Midland, National Westminster.*
Buses link St. Austell with the surrounding neighbourhood, as well as with more distant places such as Truro, Plymouth, etc. Service time-tables are displayed at key points. Terminus at Railway Station.
Bowls.—There are excellent greens at Poltair Sports Ground.
Early Closing Day.—Thursday.
Golf.—St. Austell Bay has two fine courses at Tregongeeves (Tel.: St. Austell 2649), and Crinnis (Carlyon Bay) Tel.: Par 2691. Sunday play permitted at both.
Hotels.—*Carlyon Bay; White Hart; Porth Avallen; Cliff Head; Duporth Farm.*
Licensing Hours.—10.30–2.30 and 5.30–10.30. Sundays 12–2 and 7–10.30.
Market Days.—Tuesday and Friday.
Places of Worship.—*Church of England, Methodist, Roman Catholic, Baptist, Congregational, Friends Meeting House.*
United Reformed, Friends Meeting House
Population.—32,710 (with Fowey).
Post Office.—Head Office (Night and Sunday services) in High Cross Street near the Church; sub-office at Mount Charles.
Public Library.—Carlyon Road.
Speedway.—Cornish Stadium, Par Moor, Tuesdays in summer.
Tennis.—Public courts at Poltair Recreation Ground. Also at Crinnis and Par near by.

St. Austell, an important business and residential town, is 240 miles from London and 40 miles from Plymouth. It makes a convenient headquarters for various places of interest, and its excellent and up-to-date shops give it added importance in the eyes of many visitors camping or lodging in neighbouring villages or farms.

As a Cornish town St. Austell ranks high: it is often spoken of as the richest in the county. It is pre-eminent in the China Clay industry, and the offices of clay-producing companies are on every hand.

The by-pass skirting the southern edge of the town carries most of the through traffic, but even so congestion occurs in the main street during the holiday season. Development and improvement is in progress.

Holy Trinity Church is one of the finest in the country, and its carvings have been described as "an epitome of the Creed . . . a Gospel addressed to the eye". The Perpendicular tower, which rises to a height of close on 100 feet, is ornamented with niches containing statues of the Holy Trinity, the Risen Saviour, the Virgin Mary, apostles, bishops and saints, eighteen in all; besides numerous other symbols of the Christian faith. The church contains many objects of beauty, interesting memorials and objects of historic significance, including some fine stained-glass windows, the granite and alabaster pulpit and the Shilson Memorial Baptistery. Above the western door may be seen an ancient stone clock face. This is said to be the dial of a "clok" noted in the reign of Edward VI—the only one in Cornwall at that period. Among other exterior ornaments of the building may be noted a series of fifteen escutcheons illustrating, by emblematic changes, the Passion of Our Lord.

The church itself was rebuilt in the fifteenth century, but contains portions of the three preceding styles. The font, which stands within an ornate modern baptistery, is late Norman. A number of old carved bench-ends are preserved in frames in the ringers' chamber beneath the tower, and a portion of the old rood screen may still be seen. Above the porch is a parvise chamber which, it is thought, was used in days gone by as a resting-place for travelling monks.

At the corner of Fore Street and North Street, is the **Mengue Stone,** which formerly occupied a position where three manors met, and from various circumstances was regarded with awe. It is set near the south-west wall of the church, the position being marked by a brass tablet. According to tradition, a reputed witch was burnt alive on the stone. Lake's *History* (1868) adds: "It is certain that on this stone all declarations of war and proclamations of peace were formerly read; and although at present it is partially disregarded, a strong degree of veneration still attaches to its name. All cattle that had been impounded for a given time, and for which no owner could be found, were brought to this stone and exposed for a certain number of market days, after which, if they remained unclaimed, their sale became legal."

Many Cornishmen have attained world fame by their inventions; Trevithic, Trengrouse, Humphry Davy, Bickford, to name only a few. It was at St. Austell that Joseph Hodge, the inventor of the Fire Engine, was born.

About a quarter of a mile out of the town, in the woods on the left-hand side of the Bodmin road, is the **Holy Well of**

Menacuddle and the **Stone Chair,** said to be Druidical, rough-hewn from a piece of granite, from which the well gets its name ("menacuddle" is old Cornish for "stone in a wood").

Southwards, at Trewhiddle, close to the lovely Pentewan Valley, a very important discovery of Roman and early Saxon relics was made in 1774. The hoard included an exceptionally beautiful silver chalice (said to be the oldest surviving piece of church plate), mounts for drinking horns, a silver strap-end, rings, a knotted scourge of silver wire and various other silver articles. Of priceless historical value they are in the care of the British Museum.

St. Austell is chiefly notable as the centre of—

The China Clay Industry

Probably the first thing that strikes the visitor as "different" is the scattered groups of giant, white pyramids seen to the north of the railway line near St. Austell, or noted by motorists from the London–Land's End highway, towards the south-west, shortly after topping the long hill out of Lanivet. These are the "burrows," of waste material, which has been extracted during the process of refining China Clay—that pure white, velvety substance, the production of which is not only a principal industry of the Duchy today, but is also one of our most important exports to the dollar countries.

China Clay (or Kaolin) is, in simple language, highly decomposed granite, rotted by the action of water. The outstanding properties of this substance as a potter's clay were first appreciated by the Chinese—hence

the name—who have employed it for thousands of years in the fashioning of their finest porcelain.

The discovery of China Clay deposits in Cornwall was made in 1746 by William Cookworthy, a native of Kingsbridge, Devon. Its particularly fine quality was quickly recognised by foremost British pottery concerns, but it was many years later before it was put to additional uses. Nowadays China Clay also plays an important part in numerous manufacturing processes, including the making of paper, textiles, linoleum, chemicals, cosmetics, shaving-soap, paint—and even as a base for certain medicines. With the exception of China, this part of England enjoys almost a world monopoly for the highest quality, pure white Kaolin, and the demand exceeds the supply. Output totals close on a mililion tons a year.

China Clay is obtained from open pits by directing on to the sides powerful jets of water which wash away everything in their path. The clay, together with sand, stones, etc., is carried to the bottom of the pit. After repeated washings the clay is separated from the waste, and is then pumped up to the "Micas" on the surface, where it undergoes further washing and filtering. The resulting waste is conveyed to the top of the burrow and tipped out by special apparatus.

Separated, finally, from every trace of sand and impurities, the clay is removed to the "dry," a long, one-storied building with a furnace at one end and a tall chimney at the other, by means of which the floor is heated and the surplus moisture extracted. Subsequently, through openings in the sides of the "dry," the clay is loaded directly into railway trucks or lorries for transport by rail, or to Fowey, Par or Charlestown for shipment abroad.

Some of the older pits are of considerable size, extending to 300 feet in depth and up to a mile in circumference. For every ton of pure clay recovered roughly five tons of waste finds its way to the top of the burrow. This waste, consisting mainly of quartz and sand—useless to the industry —now forms the basis of certain types of concrete and building blocks.

China Stone contains quartz and, although a good building stone, its main use is in the production of glaze for facing earthenware.

Motorists proceeding westwards will notice an isolated China Clay pit close to the right of the road when crossing Bodmin Moor on road A30. But, to pass through the heart of this industry, take the St. Austell road half-way up the hill out of Lanivet (A391).

Charlestown

(*Rashleigh Arms; Pendennis; Pier House*) is a tiny port which still secures by right of proximity a considerable part of the shipping business of the Clay Country. Its single small dock is usually busy with vessels of the smaller classes: steamships loading China Clay in bulk, grimy little colliers discharging coal. It has in recent years become popular with summer visitors, especially with people staying at the nearby Duporth Holiday Camp.

Due south of Charlestown is **Duporth Beach,** a delightfully quiet and safe spot. There is a popular holiday camp in the vicinity and other accommodation is available.

Eastward from Charlestown is **Carlyon Bay**, an attractive modern suburb with hotels (*Carlyon Bay; Cliff Head, Port Avallen*), golf links, excellent sands and facilities for sports and games of all kinds.

The road serving Carlyon Bay joins the main highway near **Biscovey,** where outside the chancel door of St. Mary's church is the *Biscovey Stone*, an inscribed granite monolith, which, although it is regarded as a decapitated cross, still rises some 8 feet out of the ground.

St. Blazey, Par, Tywardreath, Lostwithiel and other places eastward of St. Austell are described on later pages.

Mevagissey

Access.—Nearest railway station, St. Austell (Western Region Line), 5¼ miles.
Banks.—*Barclays, Lloyds, Midland.*
Buses.—Mevagissey and its neighbour Pentewan are connected with St. Austell by a regular and frequent bus service.
Car Parks.—Two in town. One on quay.
Inns.—*Ship, Fountain* and *King's Arms, Treloen, Hollies Guest House, Valley Park Guest House.*
Licensing Hours.—10.30–2.30 and 5.30–10-30. Sundays 12–2 and 7–10.30.
Post Office.—St. George's Square. Open weekdays 9 a.m.–1 p.m. and 2 p.m.–5.30 p.m. Except Saturdays 9 a.m.–1 p.m.

Since the advent of motor cars Mevagissey has grown from an old-world fishing village into a popular resort for summer visitors. Its narrow streets and devious alleyways, with cottages perched at crazy angles, remain as relics of the days when pilchard-seine fishery and smuggling were its main activities. On the steep hillsides surrounding the ancient village numerous houses have sprung up, and countless bed-and-breakfast signs meet the eye during the season. Pleasure boats, taking visitors for an hour's trip in the bay, ply constantly from the quays in summer. A building on the wharf-side, formerly the life-boat house, now serves as an attractive **aquarium.**

Seats and benches on the quays of the inner harbour accommodate holiday-makers who laze in the sunshine and watch the fishing boats or pleasure-craft go in or out, while the arms of the outer harbour provide delightful promenades. **Anglers** occupy the pier-heads, where the catch may be **mackerel, pollack, conger,** with an occasional **bass** or **turbot.**

In by-gone days huge quantities of pilchards were caught in Mevagissey seines, "cured" in rock salt, packed in casks, and exported to Italy and the West Indies. The victualling yards of the Navy also took supplies, the savoury fish being nicknamed "Mevagissey Ducks" by the seamen. The little fishing port's record output was in the year 1724, when over four thousand tons of pilchards were dispatched.

Cottages on the eastern cliff side, extending from the *Fountain Inn* to the Battery, form the most ancient part of the town.

In 1968 a **Museum** was established in one of the old boat-building workshops on the East Quay. Many of the exhibits are connected with the sea and the fishing which have been the life blood of the town. A traditional Cornish kitchen, and a large granite apple crusher and cider press attract much attention. *Open Easter to October, Weekdays from 10 a.m. Sundays from 2 p.m.*

The **Parish Church** of St. Peter, dedicated in 1259, was restored in 1887. There is an interesting memorial to Otwell Hill, dated 1617, on the north side of the chancel. A finely cut slab of Cornish slate commemorates the Dart family (1632) on the north wall of the aisle. The font is late Norman. The registers date from 1598.

Polstreath Beach, beyond the coastguard station, a favourite spot for safe bathing and picnics, is of fairly easy access, but involves a stiff climb to the cliff top on returning.

The best view of the Harbour and the town huddled between the hills at its head is from near the top of the Portmellon road, a sharp climb southward. **Portmellon** consists of a small colony at the edge of a pretty cove about a mile from Mevagissey; its little beach offers fair bathing.

Inland from Mevagissey are several small but attractive villages, all of them quite unspoilt. The largest is **St. Ewe** (*Crown Inn*) with a church approached through an avenue of palms. The screen and pulpit are well carved and the capitals of the piers between nave and south aisle are interesting. Note the size of the base of the village cross. **Polmassick** lies near the head of the valley of the little stream flowing into the sea at Porthluney (*see* p. 59)—all very pleasant country.

A mile or so northward from Mevagissey is—

Coverack Harbour

Mevagissey

Polruan, from Fowey

Fowey

Pentewan

(*Ship Inn*), in much favour with visitors who enjoy a quiet holiday. Furnished cottages and apartments are to be had. The expanse of turf bordering the shore is a popular caravan and camping site with an excellent beach.

From Pentewan a very steep and rough road (gradient 1 in 4½) climbs past the quarries and on towards **Black Head,** on the northern side of which is **Trenarren,** a delightful little village almost lost among the trees of its lovely narrow valley. Motorists should note that below the village the lane gradually narrows to a mere track and then to a footpath, with no turning-place for cars. Above the village the road has been widened to form a convenient parking place—and this is also a fine view-point. (Path to Black Head at this point.)

The nearby beach at **Hallane** is a favourite spot for picnics.

Two miles beyond Black Head and hardly more than a mile from the outskirts of St. Austell is—

Porthpean

Buses (Western National) to and from St. Austell daily.
Bathing.—Excellent; sandy beach. Car Park.

Porthpean, consisting of a small cliff-sheltered bay and a number of modern residences, is now a part of St. Austell. It is a popular little resort, and the beach is thronged with visitors in the summer. At low tide the rock pools afford fascinating interest to young and old alike. Particularly fine views are obtained from the cliff above the little bay, ranging from Gribbin Head to Chapel Point. *Coffin Cave*, on the eastern side of the sandy beach, should be seen. Good bathing, boating and fishing can be had.

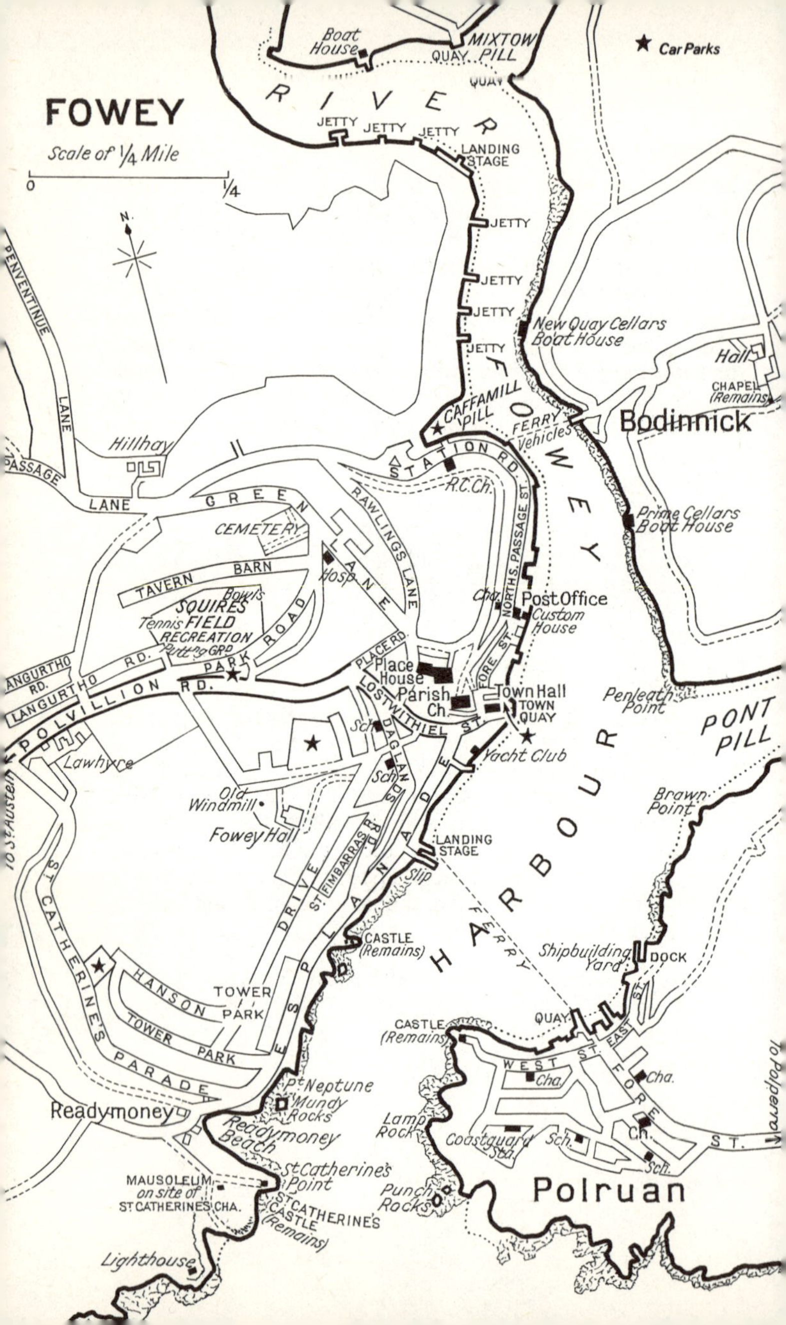

FOWEY
Scale of 1/4 Mile
0
1/4
N.
Car Parks
Boat House
MIXTOW PILL
QUAY
QUAY
RIVER
JETTY
JETTY
JETTY
LANDING STAGE
JETTY
JETTY
JETTY
JETTY
New Quay Cellars Boat House
Hall
CHAPEL (Remains)
Bodinnick
CAFFAMILL PILL
FERRY Vehicles
FOWEY
PENVENTINUE LANE
Hillhay
PASSAGE LANE
GREEN LANE
STATION RD.
R.C.Ch.
RAWLINGS LANE
NORTH S. PASSAGE ST.
CEMETERY
Hosp.
Prime Cellars Boat House
TAVERN BARN
Bowls
SQUIRES FIELD
Tennis
RECREATION
Putting GRD
PARK ROAD
Cha.
Post Office
Custom House
LANGURTHO RD.
LANGURTHO RD.
POLVILLION RD.
PLACE RD.
Place House
Parish Ch.
FORE ST.
Town Hall
TOWN QUAY
LOSTWITHIEL ST.
Penleath Point
PONT PILL
Sch.
DAGLANDS RD.
Yacht Club
Lawhyre
Sch.
HARBOUR
Old Windmill
Fowey Hall
To St. Austell
Brawn Point
LANDING STAGE
Slip
ST. FIMBARRAS RD.
DRIVE
FERRY
ESPLANADE
CASTLE (Remains)
Shipbuilding Yard
DOCK
ST. CATHERINE'S PARADE
HANSON
TOWER PARK
TOWER PARK
QUAY
CASTLE (Remains)
EAST ST.
WEST ST.
FORE ST.
Cha.
Cha.
Pt. Neptune
Mundy Rocks
Readymoney
Readymoney Beach
Lamp Rock
Coastguard Sta.
Sch.
Ch.
Sch.
To Polperro
MAUSOLEUM on site of ST. CATHERINES CHA.
St. Catherine's Point
ST. CATHERINE'S CASTLE (Remains)
Punch Rocks
Polruan
Lighthouse

Fowey and Neighbourhood

General Information

Access.—*Rail.* By Western Region Line to Par or St. Austell, thence by bus. Distance from Paddington 264¾ miles.

Road.—See pp. 11–15. Regular bus service to and from St. Austell and coach trips from all parts.

Banks.—*Barclays, Lloyds, Midland.*

Bathing.—In the absence of a large sandy beach, bathers make the best use they can of the rocks and numerous coves. At Readymoney Cove is a small sandy beach, and this is the usual resort.

Boating.—Rowing and motor boats are available for hire with or without man at recognised rates regulated by the Harbour Commissioners. Fowey Town Quay and Polruan Town Quay are usual hiring points.

Bowling Green on the Squire's Field Recreation Ground.

Buses connect Fowey with St. Austell by way of Castle Dore, Tywardreath, Par and St. Blazey and also *via* Polkerris Turning and Polmear to Par. The services between Polruan and Polperro, and Polperro and Looe are worth noting. Private bus service to and from Lostwithiel via Golant.

Car Parks on Town Quay; Park Road; Central Car Park, New Road Hill, Station Road; and above Readymoney Cove.

Distances, by road:

	Miles		*Miles*		*Miles*
Bodmin	12	London	241	Redruth	33
Carlyon Bay	6½	Looe (ferry)	10	St. Ives	50
Falmouth	36	Newquay	24½	St. Austell	9
Land's End	60	Penzance	50	Truro	23
Lizard	48				

Early Closing Day.—Wednesday

Entertainments.—Dances, etc., in the Armoury and in Town Hall.

Ferries.—There are two harbour ferries: (*a*) from Passage Slip near the Station to Bodinnick. This carries cars; (*b*) a frequent ferry for pedestrians only from Whitehouse to Polruan.

Fishing.—Excellent. Pollack and whiting can be had at any time of the year for the trouble of throwing a line overboard. Mackerel and bass are plentiful from June to September. Fowey is also noted for salmon fishing (net and rod). September and October are the favourite months. Shark fishing is also very popular. Membership to the Sea-Angling Club open to visitors.

Golf.—The 18-hole course at Carlyon Bay is within easy reach.

Hotels.—*Penlee*, Esplanade; *Riverside*, *Ashley House*, Esplanade; *Marina Villa*, Esplanade; *Old Quay House*, *Fore Street*; *The Square Rig; Greenbank*, Daglands Road; *Safe Harbour*; *Ship Inn: Rockside; Globe;* and numerous guest houses.

Library.—County Branch Library, Church Avenue.

Licensing Hours.—10.30–2.30 and 5.30–10.30. Sundays, 12–2 and 7–10.30.

Places of Worship.—*Parish Church*, 8, 11, 6.30; *United Reformed*, 11 and 6.30; *Wesleyan*, 11 and 6; *Jehovah's Witnesses*, Kingdom Hall. *Roman Catholic* (see notices).

Population.—2300.

Post Office.—Custom House Hill. Weekdays: 8.30 a.m.–5.30 p.m.

Situation.—Fowey is an ancient seaport on the south coast of Cornwall, midway between Plymouth and Falmouth, 237 miles from London, 28 miles from Plymouth and 9 miles from St. Austell. The town is built on the western side of Fowey Harbour, on rocks which rise steeply from the water.

Tennis.—Hard Courts on the Squire's Field Recreation Ground.

Yachting.—Fowey is growing in popularity year by year as a yachting centre, and a great number of fine vessels visit the port. The *Royal Fowey Yacht Club* has an excellent clubhouse. The annual Regatta, which includes Channel races, is held about the third week of August. A Regatta for all classes of yachts is held in June. The Fowey Gallants Sailing Club welcomes visitors.

Pretty little Fowey—or Foy, as it is called—disarms criticism, for it is unique. No sooner does the visitor arrive than he perceives the happy, buoyant, irresponsible tone pervading the little town. The long straggling street running parallel with the river is wide enough to accommodate a comfortable perambulator, and we naturally look to see the thoroughfare labelled "Broadway." Here we are mistaken. It is modestly called Passage Street, and the would-be captious critic, sighing for the demarcation of a footpath, indulgently smiles as he backs himself into a cottage to allow a vehicle to pass. Each street intrudes itself, apologetically, of course, so close to every other street that the ground plan is a Chinese puzzle; each house nods at every other house and says: "Well, we *are* packed—just standing room and no more." Each visitor takes up as little space as he or she can, in a friendly give-and-take spirit; and each resident says to every other resident at the height of the season: "The town is fairly full just now; it's a

wonder how we managed such a squeeze, but we have." Finally, each yacht in the harbour regards every other yacht with benevolent welcome, wondering the while at the apparent elasticity of the rock-bound haven.

Fowey Harbour is a charming inlet between imposing headlands, extending inland for 6 miles to Lostwithiel, with good depth of water for the first mile or so. This strip of water provides a safe, convenient, and picturesque anchorage for hundreds of yachts during the summer months. The most popular spot in all Fowey is the Town Quay. To the left the steep hillside at **Bodinnick** is covered from summit to water's edge in rich, dark green foliage. Opposite is the lovely wooded creek of **Pont Pill,** while, to the right lies picturesque **Polruan.** Between is the deep ultramarine of the Fowey estuary—plus all the colourful animation of a busy harbour. On a bright, morning it is, indeed, a very lovely picture.

The business of the port has grown somewhat of late, and those who cherish the theory that all the trade must go to the big ports will look with surprise upon the many door plates announcing the presence of Vice-Consulates of other countries. Vessels of 10,000 tons and more put into Fowey to receive cargoes of China clay for various parts of the world. The jetties at which the clay is shipped are well equipped, and those who do not mind being powdered with white dust will find interest in a visit to the jetty-side. The large mechanical jetty at Carne Point is capable of loading bulk clay from railway wagons into a ship's hold at the rate of 240 tons per hour. By an ingenious system of belt conveyors and a travelling tower to carry the chute, a vessel may be loaded at all her hatchways in turn without being moved at all. Lovers of beauty rejoice that the commercial portion of the river is as much out of sight as possible, beyond the former railway station.

Fowey is not now served by railway. A bus service, however, connects with Par on the main line.

The Fowey Gallants

Fowey has had a stirring history. The stories of the "Fowey Gallants" read like a romance. All the greatest sea traditions of Cornwall have their origin in Fowey and the doings of its maritime worthies. The little town is still proud to tell how, when Edward III besieged Calais, Fowey's contribution to the fleet was no less than 47 ships and 770 men. Yarmouth sent 43 ships, Dartmouth 32, and London 25! The term "Fowey Gallants" was earned by the Fowey men when they sailed by the ports of Rye and Winchelsea and "refused to vaile their bonnets" at the summons of those towns. The "Ripiers" went out to compel them, but got such "rough entertainment" that they were glad to depart without bidding farewell. (Membership of the Fowey Gallants Club is open to visitors.)

Fowey owes not a little of its popularity to a distinguished resident, "Q," otherwise Sir Arthur Quiller-Couch (d. 1944), whose novels spread the fame of "Troy Town" far and wide.

Fowey was a "freetown" as long ago as the reign of Henry II. It was incorporated in the time of James II. Up to 1684 the business of the town was conducted in the Church. It was then transferred to the Town Hall. In 1827, a writ was issued against the Corporation for the abuse of their privileges, and, judgement going against them, that finished the Corporation for the time; it was abolished under the Act of 1883. The insignia went into the possession of the Rashleigh family, and the Town Hall to the Treffrys. In November 1913, largely through the efforts of Sir Arthur Quiller-Couch and other local gentlemen, its ancient civic rights were restored to Fowey, but in recent times it has been incorporated for local government purposes with St. Austell.

From the Harbour, cruises can be taken to Gribbin Head, Polkerris, St. Austell Bay, Mevagissey, the Dodman, to the west; or to Lantivet Bay, Polperro and Looe, to the east. Within the Harbour, the possible excursions to Pont, Penpoll, Cliff, Golant, Lerryn Creek and Lostwithiel make a holiday all too short. As to the scenery and the walks, words are inadequate.

There are two striking buildings in the town, and the beautifully proportioned **Parish Church**, dedicated to St. Finnbarr (Fimbarrus) of Cork, is one.

In 1336 the church was rebuilt and re-dedicated to St. Nicholas, the patron saint of sailors, but the Fowey people soon returned to the old patron, St. Finnbarr. The lofty fifteenth-century wagon roof of the nave has still much of the original carved timber. The font is Norman (1150) of Catacleuse stone from Harlyn Bay, near Padstow. The south porch is rib-vaulted in stone and has a chamber above. The carved pulpit, said to have been made from the oak of a Spanish galleon, bears the date 1601. The monuments are of interest, notably the tomb of John Rashleigh in the north aisle, with recumbent figure in alabaster and quaint inscription. Near at hand are several small floor brasses. South of the choir is the Treffry aisle, with a number of interesting monuments. The choir screen, with its fine carvings after the manner of the fifteenth-century screens of Devonshire, is modern. The very handsome four-staged tower, which rises to a height of 119 feet, contains a clock and a peal of eight bells. There are four brasses on an east window-sill.

Place,

the seat of the Treffry family for centuries, overlooks the church. In 1457 the French, having landed at Fowey and sacked the town, were repulsed by Dame Elizabeth Treffry (in the absence of her husband) when they attacked Place. The mansion was rebuilt soon afterwards, and materially strengthened. Again, in 1740, the east front was rebuilt. Finally, in the beginning of the nineteenth century, Place was restored and practically rebuilt. The south front is battlemented. The very fine ornamentation (partly visible from Church Avenue) is similar to that which decorates the church tower. Place still retains many splendid relics of Tudor days, including a quaint chair used by Queen Elizabeth on her visit to the Bishop of Exeter. Hugh Peters, Cromwell's chaplain, was born at Fowey, his mother being a Treffry. (*House not shown.*)

The **Esplanade** is the name given to the cliff road, leading to the Harbour mouth. From the Masonic Lodge, this road passes Whitehouse Ferry and slip; "The Haven," once the house of Sir Arthur Quiller-Couch; and continues past Polly Foot's Cove and Point Neptune to Readymoney Cove (no parking) and the Battery. All the way grand views are obtained of the Harbour entrance and the picturesque little township of Polruan on the opposite side. **St. Saviour's Point,** Polruan, is now vested in the National Trust, as also are the summit and southern slopes of St. Catherine's Point. The woods and gardens above St. Catherine's or Readymoney Cove are the property of the town and are open to the public.

Just beyond *Point Neptune*, a big house, is **Readymoney Cove,** in the hollow between the Esplanade and St. Catherine's Castle. It is a pretty spot, much used for bathing.

St. Catherine's Parade is a private road (*open to pedestrians by courtesy of Sir John Hanson, Bt.*) turning inland from Point Neptune to the main road to Par, and overlooks a valley. The walk is level and pleasant.

St. Catherine's Castle (1540) is now but a small ruin, though it played an important part in the defence of the Harbour in the old days when raids were common between rival towns on either side of the Channel. The Harbour chain was held at the blockhouses, one a little farther up the river and the other at Polruan. A lovely view of the sea coast and the surrounding district is gained from the headland in which the Castle is set. The land here is now cared for by the National Trust, while the castle ruin is in the hands of the Department of the Environment (*open daily, free*).

Above the gorse on this elevation there appears what might

be taken for the top of a gigantic stone crown. It is known as the *Rashleigh Mausoleum.* Two granite arches, intersecting at right angles and surmounted by a Maltese cross, span the tombs of William Rashleigh, of Menabilly (died 1871), and his wife and daughter.

Polridmouth Cove is beyond, and a little distance farther brings us to **Gribbin Head,** with its Beacon, commanding a magnificent view (*see* pp. 106–7).

Excursions from Fowey

The range and variety of these excursions make it desirable to divide them into three classes—(*a*) by land, (*b*) by sea, (*c*) within Harbour and river, although many places can be visited equally well by boat, train, motor, or afoot.

A.—BY LAND

I. The Hall Walk and Lanteglos

The visitor has not seen Fowey until he takes the Hall Walk, which is just above Bodinnick. To continue to Lanteglos (accent on the *second* syllable) makes a round of over 4 miles. Cross the Harbour by the car ferry to **Bodinnick,** beloved of artists. Go up the steep village street about 150 yards, and take the path on the right by the old School house. Any cottager will point out the path.

The **Hall** is now a farmhouse, from the vicinity of which there is a superb view across the Harbour to Fowey. Nearly the whole of Fowey is seen. Away beyond is the granite pillar on Gribbin Head, and in the far distance looms the Dodman.

On Hall Walk are two granite memorials. One commemorating the men of Fowey and Lanteglos who fell in the 1939–45 war and the other, on Penleath Point, in memory of Sir Arthur Quiller-Couch and for which purpose the area was presented to the National Trust by Col P. F. Shakerley O.B.E.

The Hall Walk leads to a path which skirts **Pont Pill,** and presently Lanteglos Church is sighted on the other side of the creek. The path, still at the hill top, enters through a field into a private wood, though the path is public. Through the thick trees on the right glimpses can be obtained of the waters of the creek, a good distance below. The path descends to the road where turn left for an old mill. Bearing right the road continues round and back to **Pont** on the other side of the river.

From Pont it is a stiff climb to **Lanteglos Church** (*open all day*) an ancient building well worth a visit. Note the fine font, the carved bench-ends and panelling, the old wagon roofs, the old glass in the east window of south aisle, the stocks and the alabaster tablet carved in alto-relievo showing St. Lawrence's martyrdom. Among the tombs of interest special note should be made of two Mohun brasses. That of Thomas de Mohun lies in a canopied recess and depicts him clad in plate armour, a running inscription being inlaid to form a rectangular border. Spaces left for completion of the date of his death were never filled in, and the year remains MCCCC. . . . The second brass is that of John Mohun and his wife, Anne, who died in 1508. Five sons and four daughters are shown below the parents' feet.

The lantern cross outside the south door can hardly be rivalled in Cornwall. Its shaft is ornamented with quatrefoils, crosses and scrollwork. In four canopied recesses in the head appear the Virgin and Child, the Crucifixion and two other figures less easily identified. The churchyard also contains an ancient cross placed there in 1908. On the lintel post, close to the door latch may be seen a "Chi-Rho" sign thought to date from the eighth century. (*See* also p. 133).

From the church a road runs westward to join the road from Pont to Polruan. There is a pretty view of Pont Creek and hills on one side, with the sea and cliffs on the other. Polruan Quay is about 1½ miles from Lanteglos Church. The road descends steeply through the village of **Polruan**, with houses on either side. A little way down, note remains of an ancient cross and village well or fountain and, beyond, the Mission Church. From the quay, a pedestrian ferry connects with Whitehouse Slip, on the Fowey side of the Harbour.

For the country on from Lanteglos to **Polperro** and **Looe,** *see* pp. 132–4.

II. Gribbin Head

About three miles each way, *via* the Esplanade and the path which descends into Readymoney Cove. Cross the stream, and ascend by the path to the left through the woods. The ruins of St. Catherine's Castle are soon reached, with the Rashleigh Mausoleum close at hand. From this point it is possible to walk around the edge of the cliffs to Polridmouth; but those who take this route must be prepared to cross two deep "coombes." The easier way is to strike inland from the Mausoleum to a cart-track running across Allday's Fields to Coombe Farm. Keeping the farm buildings on our left we come to a crossing in the farm road. Here we turn left into a rough lane which must be followed through all its windings until it terminates before two gates. Entering the gate on the right we find ourselves in a field, with a wall on our left which will lead us down to **Polridmouth Beach.**

The lovely woods of **Menabilly** clothe the opposite hill.

The ascent of **Gribbin Head** is not difficult. The view is grand. Westward is the long, flat-topped promontory of the Dodman. Par sands and harbour lie in the bay. Fowey Harbour is to the north-east, and in the far distance Rame Head, outside Plymouth, is discernible on a clear day.

The return can be varied by way of Menabilly Barton and so to the main road, where it is possible to pick up a bus.

III. Restormel Castle

Open to public March, April, Oct.: Weekdays, 9.30–5.30, Sundays, 2–5.30. May–Sept.: 9.30–7, including Sundays. Nov.–Feb.: 10–4.30, Sundays 2–4.30.

Admission.—fee.

Approaches.—By road or water to Lostwithiel.

Distance by road, 9 miles from Fowey, 1½ from Lostwithiel (keep straight ahead into town avoiding the by-pass: *see below*).

The Castle is situated about 1½ miles due north of Lostwithiel (*see* pp. 115–17). From Lostwithiel take the road next to the Talbot Hotel. It leads along a lovely valley, thickly wooded on the left, and affording a view of the Fowey River and the main line of the railway to the right, across the meadows. After a long mile the road turns sharply to the left, uphill, leaving extensive farm buildings on the right in the corner. The castle is now easily seen across the hill, a couple of hundred yards from the road, on the right.

The earliest Castle was an earthwork consisting of a ring motte with a bailey, now largely obliterated, on the west side. This dated from the early twelfth century. About 1200 a masonry shell keep was built on top of the circular ramparts, with the curtain wall over 8 feet thick. In the late thirteenth century two-storeyed apartments surrounding the courtyard were

built inside the keep, replacing earlier wooden structures. Water was brought into the Castle through a lead conduit from the higher ground near by.

The earliest mention is in 1264 when it was surrendered, with other castles, to Simon de Montfort by Thomas de Tracy. Since 1299 it has belonged to the Earldom (later Duchy) of Cornwall. In the sixteenth century the buildings were unoccupied and ruinous. Leland wrote: "Ther is a castel on an hil in the Park of Restormel, wher sumtymes the Erles of Cornewal lay." Yet in the Civil War the keep was garrisoned by the Parliamentary army and was captured by Sir Richard Grenville on behalf of the King in 1644. Since 1925, the Castle has been in the care of the Department of the Environment.

At the foot of the hill on which the Castle stands is **Restormel House,** formerly called the Trinity, as it occupies the site of an ancient chapel dedicated to the Holy Trinity.

IV. The Luxulyan Valley

This is a region of considerable loveliness, and few visitors to this part of Cornwall fail to make an effort to see some portion, if not the whole of the valley. **Luxulyan** is a village with a railway station on the Newquay branch line from Par. By road all the way is about 9 or 10 miles each way—missing some of the best scenery. Some take train to Par and walk *up* the valley, returning from Luxulyan station.

The Luxulyan Valley is included in the itineraries of coach tours from most Cornish towns, and time is often allowed for exploration afoot.

At **Luxulyan** village (pronounced Luxilian) (*King's Arms Inn*) we are well in the granite district, and the church (dedicated to SS. Cyriac and Julitta) is the finest granite church in Cornwall. Note the huge blocks in the tower—one 7 feet 2 inches long.

The glass in the west window of the tower is sixteenth century. The pillars supporting the arches of the arcades are monoliths of granite. The Norman font (about 1150 A.D.) is particularly good, as also is the altar. The roofs of the north and south aisles show remains of the Decorated period. The documents of the ancient Stannary Parliament were kept in the turret of this church, but during the Civil War they were taken to Lostwithiel and there destroyed. A well-preserved sundial on a granite pillar stands in the churchyard.

The Roman **Well of St. Cyors** should be visited. It is close to and below the village pump, and is apt to be overlooked. The tiny Gothic "chapel" remains, but the tank in the interior was an anachronism and has been removed.

Fom the village there are several routes to the Valley. The best and by far the easiest for a stranger to find is as follows. Beyond the *King's Arms* turn right over the railway bridge and turn right again at the top of the hill. Go right through the village, passing the church on the left and down the hill. On reaching a stone bridge over a very good trout stream, turn right, then keep straight on until the Treffry Viaduct is reached. The Viaduct, 100 feet high and over 650 feet in length, was built, at a cost of £7,000, in 1839 to carry a railway (now closed) from the Treffry granite quarries and as an aqueduct. The view from above well repays the climb.

A short distance beyond the Viaduct a number of huge boulders and piles of granite, curiously poised, will be observed. The Wellington sarcophagus, in the crypt of St. Paul's, was made from a special granite found only in this valley and called Luxulyanite. It consists of large crystals of black tourmaline and pink felspar, embedded in the base of grey quartz.

Take the first small turning to the left beyond the Viaduct. This leads right through the valley (muddy and treacherous going after rain) to the site of the former waterfall which used to plunge 200 feet. The water is now piped underground to the clayworks. Nevertheless the climb up to the top is rewarding for the views it offers. From here we take the path leading along and down the hill to the China Clay works. It is a walk of about a mile and a half to Par station.

The only way to Luxulyan Valley from the St. Blazey end is by Tywardreath Highway, taking the first turning on the left at Porcupine, where there are cross-roads (*see* map). This leads to Pont's Mill, a good starting place.

The entrance to the Valley is about a quarter of a mile down. Starting from Par station take the second turning on the right, and then keep straight on to Porcupine.

V. Polkerris and Par

The walk or motor ride of about 4 miles along the high road from Fowey to Par rewards one with good views. A mile and a half out we reach **Four Turnings** (all roads round Fowey seem to arrive here), in the centre of which is an **Inscribed Stone** about 8 feet high. The defaced inscription has been read DRVSTANSI HIC JACIT CVNOWORVS FILIVS: "Drustanus here lies the son of Cunomorus." Drustanus is identified with Tristram and Cunomorus is one of the names of King Mark of Cornwall. This stone originally stood at Castle Dore (p. 114). Opposite the stone is the large gateless entrance to **Menabilly** (*see* p. 107). Continuing by the Par road (that nearest Menabilly entrance) we soon have a glimpse, across the valley on our right, of *Trenython* mansion in a commanding position on the hill. This property has been acquired by the *Railwaymen's Convalescent Homes Association* and converted for their use.

On the left is the turning for the well-wooded, crescent-shaped cove of **Polkerris** (*Rashleigh Inn*), where a diminutive stone pier shelters a good sandy beach. At one time fishing was the predominant industry at Polkerris, and the old fish cellars remain. There are tea-gardens and other attractions for holiday-makers, and this is a favourite spot for picnics. The old life-boat house is now a café.

From Polkerris turning the main road goes down Polmear hill on the way to Par. We pass, on the right, another inscribed stone (with surrounding stone seat), but this is modern and records the grateful thanks to Heaven of "J.R." (Jonathan Rashleigh, of Menabilly) for the preservation of his life when thrown from his horse last century.

Par Sands (*Ship Inn:* at Par—*Royal, Haven*) soon open out with a grand marine view. At low water there is a very extensive flat beach of good sand, and a number of bathing-huts, tennis courts, model-yacht pools, bowling greens, and a café help to increase the ever-rising popularity of the place. The Harbour is small, but has a flourishing and busy trade. Coal is brought and China Clay, stone and granite shipped in large quantities. **Spit Beach,** west of the Harbour, is a popular place for picnics.

On the hills inland stands the village of **Tywardreath.** The Manor of Tiwardrai is recorded in the Exeter Domesday. St. Andrew's Priory, which stood just below the present churchyard, was founded about A.D. 1150 by monks from Angers in Normandy but it has now disappeared. St. Andrew's Church dates from 1347. Much of interest was lost when the church was largely rebuilt in 1880. The tower, which is original, dates from 1480, and contains a ring of six bells, first hung in 1774, re-hung in 1949, but never recast. The tombstone of Thomas Colyns, last Prior of St. Andrew's Priory, is attached to the wall of the north transept. It was formerly in the chancel floor. The pulpit is made of ancient carved bench-ends and others are in the pew ends in the transept. The Altar stone which was found at the restoration of 1880 is medieval. Four consecration crosses are still visible in it. The church records go back to 1642.

Not far from Par is **St. Blazey,** close to which on higher ground, will be noticed a pretty square embattled tower, covered with ivy. This stands in the grounds of **Scobell,** now in use as a private school. The sea within the last century extended beyond the grounds of Scobell and St. Blazey station, and it will be noticed how low-lying is some of the ground. The sea was forced back by deposits brought down by the river Par. The village of St. Blazey lies beyond the station, but is not of particular interest. Visitors who do get so far should, however, enter the fourteenth-century Church of St. Blaise, Bishop and Martyr. Near St. Blazey was born the celebrated *Ralph Allen* of Bath, who, in the early eighteenth century reformed the postal system of England, and introduced the first cheap cross-country post.

B.—WATER TRIPS FROM FOWEY

It is to the water that everyone at Fowey looks for occupation, business and pleasure; and boating is the chief pursuit. With the exception of Falmouth, no holiday resort in Cornwall offers a greater variety of water excursions. Outside the Harbour, the coast-line, rocky and grand in the extreme, is intersected by little ravines lined with tiny fishing villages, each unlike the others; while the creeks of the Harbour, with their lake-like surfaces, are irresistibly attractive to the lover of boating.

For all excursions by sea a boatman should be taken, unless the person in charge of the boat has a good knowledge of local currents and tides.

I. **To Polperro.** About 6 miles east. Clearing the Harbour, we pass Blackbottle Head, a perpendicular cliff about 400 feet high. Passing Lantic Bay to port, we round Pencarrow Head. Lantivet Bay comes next, and after a stretch of about 3 miles of cliff we draw in for **Polperro,** one of the prettiest and quaintest little coves on the coast (*see* pp. 135–8).

II. **To Looe.** About 10 miles. We pass Polperro, with its white modern houses on the cliff, cross Talland Bay, and passing inside Looe Island (or rounding the Ranneys rocks of its south-east corner, according to the state of the tide) alter our eastern course for north. There is a convenient pier for landing. Looe is described on pp. 120–3.

III. **To Polridmouth.** One mile to the south-west. This is the shortest sea trip from Fowey and is very popular on a summer afternoon. The scenery is pretty around Polridmouth Bay, quiet and sheltered by bold Gribbin Head. It is usual to land (by running the boat on the beach), and climb Gribbin head.

IV. **To Polkerris, Par Sands and Porthpean.** Gribbin Head separates St. Austell Bay from Fowey waters. After rounding the Gribbin, we pass another fine cliff called Little Gribbin. **Polkerris** (*see* p. 110) lies 1½ miles up the Bay. Passing Fishing Point, Carlyon Beach and Landrion Point we come to **Charlestown,** the port for St. Austell, a couple of miles inland. Cruising down the west side of St. Austell Bay we reach **Porthpean,** a small but thriving holiday resort due for further development (*see* p. 97).

V. **To Mevagissey.** About 7 sea miles. This is a trip right across St. Austell Bay, after passing the Gribbin. It makes an exceedingly pleasant excursion on a fine day. The small fishing town of Mevagissey is very interesting (*see* pp. 95–7).

Readymoney Cove, Fowey

The Bridge at Looe

Looe

Polperro

C.—EXCURSIONS WITHIN THE HARBOUR

The following excursions are still by water, but within the Harbour, and it is perhaps by these delightful river trips that Fowey principally endears itself to visitors.

VI. **To Pont Pill.** This is the creek opposite Whitehouse. The water winds between green and wooded hills, and the scene is one of quiet beauty. **Pont,** a little hamlet and bridge, which bars further progress, is about a mile from the Harbour. This is a favourite evening pull with those fond of rowing. Lanteglos Church, on the hill to the right, should certainly be visited (*see* p. 106).

VII. **The Lerryn River.** The Fowey River as far as Cliff is described in the next excursion. The distance from Fowey to Lerryn is 4½ miles.

After passing Cliff on the right and leaving the Lostwithiel branch on the left, Lerryn River is entered. Those unacquainted with the river need to be told that the "lake," or deep part of the course, is always on the side that has the steeper bank. Where the land slopes gradually to the water's edge the stream is shallow. The Lerryn Creek is generally considered the most delightful part of the whole estuary. The course winds through a luxuriance of beautiful woodland scenes until a turn brings the quaint old-world village of **Lerryn** into view.

According to an old couplet passed down from generation to generation in the neighbourhood—

> "One day the Devil, having nothing to do.
> Built a great hedge from Lerryn to Looe."

In Cornwall a "hedge" is no mere fence of shrubs or trees, but a good stone wall, sometimes covered with earth. The earthwork to which the lines refer may still be traced in many parts of its course across country—notably on the hillsides between Lerryn and Lanreath. Its modern name is "The *Giant's* Hedge," but its purpose remains a matter of conjecture.

VIII. **To Lostwithiel.** About 6 miles. For rowing boats, even those aided with a lug-sail, this is an ambitious trip, and many prefer to use a motor boat, but without doubt it includes the finest scenery near Fowey. The river is tidal to Lostwithiel. When proceeding beyond Golant careful attention should be paid to the tide. To go up and return with the tide gives, of course, a minimum of work. When the water is not high, the large sandbank opposite Golant should be avoided, also the treacherous mud-bank just below St. Winnow Church.

Starting from Whitehouse, we pass the ferry at **Bodinnick,** with the quaint little village built on either side of the steep lane. As we thread our way between the many vessels receiving China Clay, we have a good view of the huge mechanical conveyors on the jetties, but careful steering will be necessary. We soon have a series of delightful river vistas. On the right is the wide **Penpoll Creek,** up which, at high tide, one can row for a mile to **Penpoll,** from which a short climb leads to **St. Veep.** The Church of St. Veep was reconstructed in 1336 and rededicated to SS. Ciricus and Julitta. It has a fine old font and some good wood-carving. The oldest monument is that of Nicholas Courtenay, 1589. The registers date from 1558. On the left is a charming little creek that we must not pass without seeing. It leads to the *Saw Mill*, and the thickly-wooded hills and mirror-like waters have a great fascination for artists.

Half a mile beyond is **Golant,** sheltering under the hill. Some terraced houses and modern bungalows tend to spoil its former pretty aspect. Warwick "the Kingmaker" once lived in the parish. It is usual to halt at Golant for a walk through the village. St. Sampson's Church nestles in the shoulder of the northern hill. This, the parish church of Golant, was restored in 1509. It contains much of interest despite the "restoration" of 1842. Note the holy well beside the porch; well-preserved carved oak in pulpit, reading-desk, choir and beautiful roof, and some old glass in the north-east window.

Half a mile west of St. Sampson's Church is **Castle Dore,** an Iron Age fort which became the palace of King Mark, the uncle of Tristram and *possibly* a meeting-place of the Knights of the Round Table. It was the reputed burial-place of Tristram and Isolde. The site was carefully examined a few years ago and signs were found of three distinct occupations—300–250 B.C., A.D. 50–100 and sixth century A.D.

Cliff, on the opposite side of the river, is a favourite camping spot. The creek leading away to the right, beyond Cliff, is the **Lerryn River** (p. 113), a delightful stretch of water.

On the left, as the river branches towards Lostwithiel, is the mansion of *Penquite*. We soon come in sight of that lovely spot around **St. Winnow Church,** which is close to the water's edge. Time should be found for a glance at the building, which is late fifteenth-century on Norman remains. The old bench ends are very quaint and there are two 16th century windows. The screen is a fine example, and the pulpit a good piece of carving in arabesque design. Notice the window and brass tablet to the memory of Lieutenant Melvill who, with Lieutenant Coghill, died to save the Queen's Colours at the battle of Isandlwana.

Above St. Winnow the water narrows considerably as it approaches **Lostwithiel.** On returning the tide should, of course, be watched, not only to avoid pulling against stream, but to prevent the boat being stranded on a sandbank.

Lostwithiel

Access.—Lostwithiel Station, on Western Region main line or Bodmin Road.
For *Road Routes* see Motoring Section.
Angling.—For salmon, sea trout, brown trout, in the River Fowey. For licences apply Fernley Pearce, 7 Queen Street. Licences also obtainable for fishing on preserves of Lostwithiel Fishing Association.
Banks.—*Barclays* (Queen Street), *Lloyds* (Fore Street).
Bowls.—Restormel Road (open to visitors).
Buses.—Through Lostwithiel *en route* between Okehampton and Truro, *via* Tavistock, Callington, Liskeard, St. Blazey, St. Austell, Grampound, Probus, etc. Also to Bodmin and Wadebridge.
Car Parks.—Town Quay and Cattle Market.
Distances.—London, 239; Truro, 23; Bodmin, 6; St. Austell, 9; Fowey, 7.
Early Closing Day.—Wednesday or Saturday.
Hotels.—*Royal Talbot*, North Street; *King's Arms*, Fore Street; *Monmouth*. Parade Square; *Globe*, North Street, *Royal Oak*, Duke Street; *Carotel*, Edgcumbe Road.
Library.—County Branch Library, Municipal Offices.
Licensing Hours.—10.30–2.30 and 5.30–10.30. Sundays, 12–2 and 7–10.30.
Places of Worship.—With hours of Sunday Services: *St. Bartholomew's (Parish) Church*—8, 11 and 6.15. *Methodist*, 11 and 6.15.
Population.—1,910.
Post Office.—G.P.O., Queen Street.

Although the picturesque old town of Lostwithiel is much visited, its regular *clientèle* consists chiefly of anglers, for the "fishfull river of Foy," as Carew has it, is celebrated for its salmon and trout. To tourists and holiday-makers one of the most attractive features is **Restormel Castle,** a mile or so to the north (*see* pp. 107–8). Between Lostwithiel station and the Church is the fine **Old Bridge,** (probably thirteenth century) of nine arches, with much appreciated angular recesses on either side for the protection of foot-passengers. Instructions are given for the repair of the bridge in the Register of the Black Prince, the first Duke of Cornwall (1357). The bridge and its vicinity make a very pleasant loitering-place; though motorists find the bridge none too wide, and welcome the by-pass crossing the river by a modern bridge ¼-mile upstream.

The old *Duchy Palace* was the ancient Exchequer, Shire Hall and Stannary Prison. It dates from about 1280. The building has been restored, and is now used for Masonic purposes.

St. Bartholomew's Church has a graceful octagonal spire dating from the thirteenth century and called by G. E. Street, "the pre-eminent glory of Cornwall." Near the south porch is a medieval cross with a fine head, restored in 1882. The font, of Pentewan stone, is remarkably carved. Close by is a carved wooden pedestal on which stands the alms-box, dated 1645. In a south window will be noticed an alabaster carving, coloured, representing the flaying of St. Bartholomew. The east window, which remained undamaged by the explosion recorded below, is Early English work, and of unusual size: 34 feet by 14 feet.

The memorials and monuments are of much interest. Against the north wall is a brass effigy in armour representing one Tristram Curteys (date 1423). Note in the outside of the south wall the two sepulchral recesses. It is supposed that here were buried Robert de Cardinham and his wife (about 1225). The parish stocks, of seven holes, are preserved in the south porch. Lostwithiel Church should not on any account be missed.

The region round Lostwithiel was greatly disturbed during the Civil War, and the town was the temporary headquarters of the Parliamentarians. Some of their doings are recorded in the "Diary of Richard Symonds, one of the King's Lieutenants."

"One of their actions while they were at Listithiel must not be forgotten. In contempt of Christianity, Religion, and the Church, they brought a horse to the font in the Church, and there with their kind of ceremonies did, as they call it, christen the horse, and call him by the name of Charles, in contempt of his Sacred Majesty.

"Another was done by their Provost Martiall, who put his prisoners in the said Church. The night they marched away, two of the prisoners, being rich men of Cornwall, gott up in the steeple and pulled up the ladder, and called to the Marshall, jeering him. 'Ile fetch you downe,' said he, and sett match and hay on fire under them; besides they shott their muskets into the belfry at them; all would not doe. Then he fetch a barrel of powder and gave fire to it, threatening to blow them up, and that blew into the church and blew off most of the slate, and yet did no hurt to the prisoners."

The **Guildhall** was erected in 1740. The Town Regalia and Insignia are most interesting, including a Silver Mace and a Silver Oar, both of 1670. Lostwithiel is an ancient town, its first charter having been granted in 1189. Visitors who wish to inspect the Guildhall should apply to the Municipal Offices.

opposite. The celebrated Silas Titus, author of *Killing noe Murder*, was M.P. for Lostwithiel 1663–79.

A few yards below the Talbot Hotel is a shop bearing a curious old tablet stating that "Walter Kendal founded this house and hath a lease for 3,000 years which had beginning Sept. 29, 1652."

Beyond Restormel (*see* pp. 107–8) and 3½ miles northward of Lostwithiel is **Lanhydrock House,** the property of the National Trust, to which it was given in 1953 by Viscount Clifden, who lived here. The fine avenue was planted in 1648. Part of the house is of the Tudor period, but the greater part of the old mansion was destroyed by fire and rebuilt with additions in the 'eighties of last century. It stands in a park of 366 acres. The barbican, or principal entrance, is a fine battlemented structure bearing date 1651. The picture gallery, in the original north wing, has a remarkable plaster ceiling, depicting scenes from the Old Testament. There are formal gardens, originally laid out in 1857, with a number of bronze urns from the Chateau de Bagatelle by Louise Ballin, goldsmith to Louis XIV. *The Garden and Gallery are open daily from* 2–6 *p.m. from April–mid–October* (*admission fee*). *The park and woodlands are always open.*

The **Church of St. Hydrock** is behind the mansion. It comprises fifteenth-century work, Perpendicular style. A notable memorial is that to George Carminow, 1599, with the arms of the family and the Cornish motto: "Cala rag whethlow"—a straw for a tale-bearer.

Boconnoc lies in the charming valley of the Lerryn, 4 miles eastward from Lostwithiel. The mansion is interesting as the home of the elder Pitt in his boyhood. Boconnoc Church was renewed and dedicated in 1321, but the present fabric dates from the fifteenth century. **Braddock Down** was the scene of a battle in 1643 between the Parliamentary and Royalist forces. Not far from the house is an obelisk marking the place where the Royalists had a fort, but the obelisk is really a memorial to Sir Richard Lyttleton. Boconnoc is numbered among the finest estates in Cornwall, and was purchased by Governor Pitt with half the proceeds of the Pitt diamond, which stone he bought for £20,400, and sold to the French for £135,000. *The estate is not generally open to the public.*

The **Fowey Valley,** north of Lostwithiel, boasts some glorious scenery. The superb Valley Drive between Bodmin Road and Doublebois may be combined with a visit to Lanhydrock or Boconnoc.

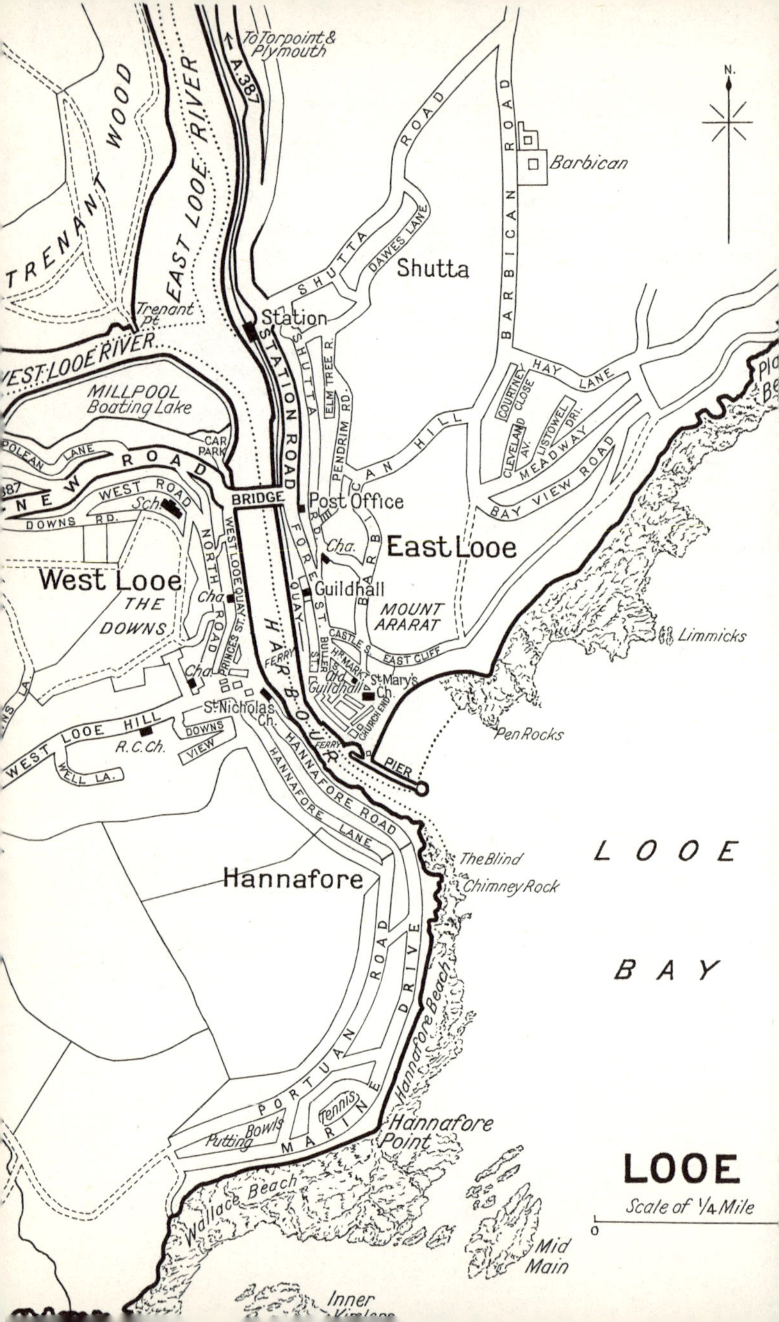

To Torpoint & Plymouth
A.387
TRENANT WOOD
EAST LOOE RIVER
Trenant Pt.
WEST LOOE RIVER
MILLPOOL Boating Lake
CAR PARK
POLEAN LANE
NEW ROAD
WEST ROAD
Sch.
DOWNS RD.
West Looe
THE DOWNS
NORTH ROAD
WEST LOOE QUAY ST.
PRINCES SQ.
Cha.
St. Nicholas Ch.
WEST LOOE HILL
R.C.Ch.
DOWNS VIEW
WELL LA.
BRIDGE
HARBOUR
FERRY
Station
STATION ROAD
SHUTTA ROAD
SHUTTA
DAWES LANE
Shutta
ELM TREE R.
PENDRIM RD.
BARBICAN HILL
BARBICAN ROAD
Barbican
Post Office
FORE ST.
QUAY
Cha.
East Looe
Guildhall
MOUNT ARARAT
CASTLE S.
EAST CLIFF
BULLER ST.
HR. MARKT.
Old Guildhall
St. Mary's Ch.
CHURCH END
PIER
HAY LANE
COURTNEY CLOSE
CLEVELAND AV.
LISTOWEL DRI.
MEADWAY
BAY VIEW ROAD
Limmicks
Pen Rocks
HANNAFORE ROAD
HANNAFORE LANE
Hannafore
The Blind
Chimney Rock
LOOE BAY
PORTUAN ROAD
MARINE DRIVE
Hannafore Beach
Tennis
Bowls
Putting
Hannafore Point
Wallace Beach
Mid Main
Inner
LOOE
Scale of 1/4 Mile
0
N.

Looe

General Information

Access.—*Road Routes: see* pp. 11–15. *Rail.* By Western Region line *via* Liskeard. There is a good service of trains and the main-line connections are good, Looe being within 6½ hours of London.

Looe is also connected with Plymouth, via Tamar Bridge or Torpoint (ferry for Plymouth), Liskeard, Polperro and Bodinnick (ferry for Fowey), by regular bus services.

Amusements and Sports Facilities

Bathing good and safe, from sand or rocks. Beach tents may be hired.

Boating on both sea and river is excellent. Rowing and motor boats may be hired at moderate rates. *Boating Lake* just above bridge. Daily cruises to Polperro, Fowey and Mevagissey.

Bowling Green and two *Putting Greens* on Hannafore sea front.

Fishing for a variety of sporting sea fish, including shark, according to season. Freshwater fishing in the Looe rivers and other streams within easy reach.

Golf: 18-hole course at Bin Down.

Hunting: East Cornwall Foxhounds, Trethill Harriers and Dartmoor Otter Hounds hunt in the district.

Tennis: Looe and Hannafore Lawn Tennis Club has courts beside the sea at Hannafore (grass and hard).

Banks.—*Barclays, Lloyds, Midland,* all in Fore Street, East Looe.

Buses.—Services to Torpoint (for Plymouth), Plymouth via Saltash and Tamar Bridge and Polperro.

Early Closing Day.—Thursday.

Hotels.—*Hannafore Point,* Marine Drive; *Annaclone; Bodrigan; Portbyhan; Rock Towers; Trevanion; Fieldhead; Kabo; Westor;* all in West Looe.

Boscarn; Ship; Looe; Deganwy; Riverside, all in East Looe.

Plaidy Beach, Plaidy Beach.

Library.—County Branch Library, Higher Market Street.

Licensing Hours.—10.30–2.30 and 5.30–11. Sundays, 12–2 and 7–10.30.

Motorists will find ample accommodation. Parking grounds are

Buller Quay and a space at Church End, beside the Pier and Beach; the former is preferable, as avoiding the necessity for taking vehicles through narrow streets in the old Town. There are also car parks on the West Quay and at the Millpool boating lake on Riverside.

Newspapers.—The daily paper of the district is the *Western Morning News* (Plymouth), and the local weeklies are the *Cornish Times* (Liskeard) and *Cornish Guardian* (Bodmin).

Places of Worship, with hours of Sunday services:

East Looe: *St. Mary's* (Parish Church)—11.15 and 6.30

West Looe: *St. Nicholas*—8 a.m.

United Reformed and *Methodist:* Riverside United Church, West Looe Quay—11 and 8.15 p.m., summer.

Roman Catholic (Our Lady and St. Nicholas)—8 and 10.

Sclerder Abbey, Talland, between Looe and Polperro—11. 10.30 in winter.

Toc H, Millpool. First Sunday at 2.45 p.m.

Population.—4,060.

Post Office.—Fore Street. Sub-Post Offices in Barbican Road, East Looe and The Quay, West Looe.

Railway Station.—Looe, Western Region Line.

The flourishing little town of Looe existed for centuries apart by itself, never troubling the rest of the county with its existence, and undisturbed save during the summer months when it welcomed its regular contingent of visitors.

In the roll of Edward III's fleet before Calais the Port of Looe is said to have sent 20 ships and 315 sailors—only 5 ships fewer than London. Long before the reign of Queen Bess Looe possessed a Mayor and free burgesses, and a charter granted in Armada year made "nine of the more honest" chief burgesses. For centuries prior to 1832 East and West Looe each returned two Members to Parliament. The Corporation records go back 500 years. West Looe was incorporated by a charter of Queen Elizabeth in 1574, but the Corporation became extinct in 1869. The East Looe Corporation met for the last time in 1886, and in the years 1873 and 1890 respectively schemes were promulgated by the Charity Commissioners for the establishment of Town Trusts to administer the Corporate properties. The Trustees for East Looe are now the Town Council, and the insignia, comprising two maces and a seal (1685–98), are in their custody.

The towns of East and West Looe are built on opposite sides of a deep river valley, so steep-sided as almost to warrant use of the word "gorge." Beyond the towns the waterway

widens to lake-like proportions and in two streams wanders inland between high hills for nearly 3 miles.

The Looes are of nearly equal antiquity, but West Looe is of considerably less commercial importance than its fellow. A picturesque granite **Bridge** of seven main arches crosses the Harbour and connects the two towns, incidentally providing a superb view. A hundred yards below this there stood an earlier bridge, having fifteen arches, with an oratory to St. Anne in the middle, which was erected in the early years of the fifteenth century, and was only superseded in 1855.

Worthy of special notice in Looe is the **Old Guildhall,** with its stone stairs and wooden balustrade leading up to the large room where the free burgesses of East Looe formerly deliberated and where may be seen the ancient stocks. This place is now a museum open to the public. High up under the porch roof is the pillory, one of the few examples remaining in the country. Between the Old Guildhall and the Bridge is the modern **Guildhall,** with clock tower. At Quay Head there is a marine aquarium of some interest, the exhibits including shark caught in Looe waters.

In Fore Street, too, close by, may be seen one of Looe's many charming examples of the domestic architecture of past centuries. The house in question was for many years the residence of Thomas Bond (1765–1837), the historian of Looe and for nearly forty years Town Clerk of both East and West Looe. It contains a fine panelled room and other interesting pieces of antique house decoration: over a fireplace is the date 1652. Of this house it is related on good authority that Davies Gilbert, P.R.S., who was Bond's residuary legatee, found in a cupboard after the latter's death no less a sum than ten thousand guineas in gold, which he caused to be conveyed to Liskeard in a farm vehicle—probably the most valuable cart-load that has yet passed over that road. The house is now a café.

But there are houses as old as Bond's on every hand. In the antique shop opposite, for instance, a stone slab with raised figures bearing the date 1666, was uncovered during restoration. The streets of Looe are extraordinarily narrow and crooked. The whole place is delightful and almost indescribable.

At **Church End,** the seaward extremity of East Looe, is Looe **Parish Church,** standing upon the site of a chapel dedicated to St. Mary in the year 1259. Beyond the Church is a **Car Park,** and beyond that the **Promenade,** overlooking a sandy beach, the most popular bathing-place. To the right the stone **Pier,** known from its shape as "The Banjo," forms the eastern arm of the Harbour entrance and provides an agreeable lounge and look-out. Hours—days—can be spent watching the boats passing in and out, the water flowing swiftly through the narrow channel and making a delicious picture before the rocky cliff along which the tree-shaded Hannafore road is carried on viaducts with battlemented turrets. The curious, steep and narrow streets in the older parts of the town will tempt visitors to while away much time.

The street-plan of **West Looe** is less involved than that of its neighbour, but there is plenty to see.

The most interesting building is the curious little quayside **Church of St. Nicholas.** The exact date of erection is unknown, but when its endowment was confirmed in 1336, upon the prayer of Sir John Dawney, it was referred to as having been built by the ancestors of that knight. In 1400 it was licensed as a chapel-of-ease for the people of West Looe, subject to preservation of the rights of the Parish Church of Talland. The endowment disappeared about the period of the Reformation and the fabric might, perhaps, have shared its fate had not Queen Elizabeth's charter of 1574 made provision for a Council Hall. To this purpose it was gradually adapted, and as Guildhall, Justice-Room and (occasionally) schoolroom it continued to serve until restored to ecclesiastical use in 1852. It then underwent considerable alteration and improvement. Reference must be made to the sunken vestry and the chancel rafters, made from timbers of the Spanish first-rate *San Josef*, captured by Nelson at the Battle of St. Vincent.

From the Church a picturesque cliff road, affording charming views, runs around the hill to **Hannafore,** a pleasant residential area facing the open sea. Those who know only Looe in the valley will be surprised at this attractive modern suburb with its extensive views over the sea and along the coast. At low tide the rocky foreshore is a grand place for juvenile crab-hunters and shrimpers. A ferry from Church End obviates the necessity of walking through both towns *via* the Bridge to reach Hannafore from East Looe.

Half a mile due south from Hannafore Point rises **Looe Island** (*see* below).

The **Harbour,** as far as the Bridge, often presents a busy scene. Here are seen numerous large fishing-luggers, for Looe is one of the principal fishing ports of Cornwall, and these little craft, with their tremendously long lines, their drift-nets or trawls, are to visitors a source of unlimited interest.

Above the Bridge the valley widens, and the waters, calm and placid, have the appearance of a lake. This feature is generally supposed to have imparted its name to the town; for the Cornish *Looe* has a similar signification to the Gaelic *Loch* and the Erse *Lough*. The steep hills, clad from summit to base in verdure, are reflected in this natural mirror and present a picture of great beauty. Opposite the Station the West Looe, or Trelawney, river comes to meet the eastern stream, and is constricted near the junction by a widely-circuitous Mill-Pool Wall, built by means of a grant from the West Looe Corporation in 1614. Here is a **Boating Lake** and an extensive car park.

Looe Island. Looe Island lies half a mile south of Hannafore Point. It is about three-quarters of a mile in circumference and about

150 feet high. A chapel (variously said to be dedicated to St. Michael, St. Nicholas and St. George), and a three-gun battery stood upon the hill, but both have disappeared. A family named Finn lived here for nearly forty years, and are credited with having exterminated its swarms of rabbits and rats by eating them indiscriminately. Many tales are told, both stirring and amusing, of the Island when it was used as a smugglers' *cache*. Looe and Polperro men were great adepts at cheating the revenue, and Looe Bay has witnessed many a sharp skirmish between adherents and infractors of the customs laws.

RIVER TRIPS

The tidal creeks of the East and West Looe rivers offer, perhaps, the most charming and most popular excursions of all from this most delightful of tourist centres. No visitor should quit the town before journeying once at least up either valley. The trip is best made in a small boat. Attention should be paid to tides.

The **West River** winds in a north-westerly direction between lofty hills for some 2 miles from Looe Bridge, until **Watergate** is reached, a few picturesque cottages surrounded by thick woodlands at the opening of a delightful side valley.

From Watergate the boat may be taken a further half-mile upstream to the point where a by-road comes down to a ford, and even then further progress is possible for those who do not shrink from the embrace of overhanging trees.

Arrived at this point, one may spend a pleasant hour in visiting **St. Nun's Well,** a little way up the valley. Leaving the boat on the western bank at the ford and crossing a tributary stream at Trelawney Mill we come soon to *Sowden's Bridge*, which is left upon our right hand. The road now begins to rise, revealing as it goes a further vista of this most charming valley. Where the highway wheels sharply upon itself we turn right into a farm road marked "Hobb Park," and a moment later over a gateway (R) into a field. The well is now immediately below us on the left, built into a bank in the angle formed by two hedges. A little rectangular porch leads into a tiny vaulted well chamber which yet allows the tallest of men to stand upright with ease.

Sometimes referred to as St. Ninnie's or The Piskie's, this ancient well is dedicated to that Nun, or Non, who was the mother of St. David. Unfortunately there is direct conflict between different accounts of both her paternity and that of her canonised son; but all agree that she was very lovely and every good Cornishman believes that she was the daughter of a local chieftain, was espoused by one of Britain's most famous Kings, and lies buried in her chapel at Altarnun, near the spot where her babe was born. Another chapel dedicated to her stood originally on the hillside above this well. Once so deeply venerated, the well is now neglected, though Nature has done her best to compensate for the shortcomings of humanity by decking the tiny building with ferns, lichens, mosses and wild flowers. It is said that when a farmer of a past age yoked his oxen to the octahedral well basin which had taken his fancy, the latter broke away and, rolling downhill, returned miraculously to its former situation. Moreover, misfortune overtook the farmer and his oxen. It would appear, however, that more recently someone has accomplished the same deed, for the basin has now gone and only a little circular trough remains upon the floor.

The visitor may descend the steep field and regain the road near Sowden's Bridge by a riverside footpath.

The **Eastern Valley** (Looe River) runs more or less due north for a mile and a half to **Terras,** where by means of a causeway between two quaint little hump-backed bridges a road crosses the water to join the riverside highway. It is worth disembarking here for a moment to glance at the little lake which lies within the lodge gates to *Trenant Park*. Motionless beneath the hanging woods, its surface aglow with water-lilies, it is the very "dark and stilly pool" of many a poet's imagination.

Above this point the river winds for an equal distance until the hamlet of **Sandplace** is reached, with its thatched cottages scattered over the hillside. Near Sandplace railway station the river passes through a culvert beneath the main road. When the tides are near spring a boat may be easily taken through this tunnel and some distance beyond. But the voyager should land here and explore. Whether he climbs **Tregarland Tor** (450 ft.) on the east (p. 128), follows the steep high road towards **Duloe** on the west, or pursues for a little while the valley road beside the stream, he will be richly repaid for his trouble.

SEA TRIPS FROM LOOE

The neighbouring coastline is so beautiful that every visitor should make a few cruises. For fishing and other purposes near the Harbour a great number of rowing and motor boats are available. In calm weather nothing is more pleasant than to hire a boat, pack it with provisions, cushions and whatever paraphernalia one may fancy, and idle up or down the coast to some stretch of open beach or tiny secluded cove where, in almost tropical sunshine, an idyllic day may be spent in bathing, fishing, prawning or exploring. Any of the beaches between Downderry and Talland may be used in this way; but it should be remembered that if the wind is southerly there will be a surf breaking—more or less according to situation—which may make landing and re-embarkation difficult. *In all cases the boatman's advice should be carefully followed.*

For long distances there are a very fine fleet of motor craft, both open launches and cabin cruisers, of the most comfortable and seaworthy construction, which make frequent trips over a wide area. A few of the more popular excursions are as follows:

1. **To Polperro** (about 4 sea miles). On leaving Looe we turn westward past Hannafore Point and Looe Island, and crossing *Portnadler Bay* we soon bring *Horestone Head* (Talland Head of the old cartographers) abeam and notice on its western slopes the first pair of black-and-white beacons marking the Naval "measured mile." As we cross the little Bay the tower of Talland Church peeps at us over the shoulder of the hill. On nearing Downend Point we note at the head of a precipice a most impressively simple War Memorial: a simple granite cross to the men of Polperro, perched in splendid isolation beside the cliff path, nearly 200 feet above the sea.

After running along under the towering cliffs, we turn in between white-fringed rocks to a harbour entrance so narrow that it may be (and sometimes is) closed against storms by baulks of timber lowered into slots in the granite piers. Here are numerous fishing boats, including a number of longliners, which constitute the local fishing fleet and above, the quaintest village in England. (For **Polperro,** *see* pp. 135–8.)

2. **To Fowey** (about 10 miles). After passing Polperro we follow the rocky coast line until we reach Nealand Point, with its overhanging cliff, and Larrick Rock. **Lantivet Bay** opens to starboard, and when we have passed the Udder Rock, with its bell-buoy and whitewashed beacon on shore, Lansallos Church soon appears from behind the eastern hill. Noticing the tiny white watch-house built about a century ago to discourage smugglers, with whom the Bay was a prime favourite, we come abreast of Pencarrow Head and crossing Lantic Bay run around St. Saviour's Point by Polruan into **Fowey** harbour (*see* pp. 101–2).

From Fowey the voyage is often extended, either for 8 miles past Gribbin Head, with its beacon pillar of granite (80 ft.), St. Austell

Bay and Black Head to **Mevagissey**; or for 4 miles up the Fowey river to the lovely village of **Lerryn** (*see* p. 113).

3. **Eastward** from Looe the coast line is equally pretty and bold, but in places less rocky. The points of interest in a voyage along this shore, though seen from a different aspect, are almost entirely identical with those to be noted in walking from Looe to Rame Head by the cliff-road; and we may therefore safely refer the reader to pp. 139–144. East of Plaidy and Millendreath beaches, landing is possible at Seaton, Downderry, Portwrinkle and certain spots beyond.

4. A favourite sea trip in fine weather is a visit to the **Eddystone** (*see* p. 144), where visitors may land if the sea is kind, and are permitted to inspect the lighthouse. From Looe the rocks bear nearly south-south-east, distant about 13 sea miles; and the run out to sea, with the land falling away on either hand, is most enjoyable. One passes close to the bell-buoy on the Knight-Errant Patch, the extremity of a ridge of rocky shallows running out from Downderry.

Walks Around Looe

I. To St. Martin, Morval and Sandplace

Distance.—4½ miles.

Leaving Looe by the St. Martin's Road, Shutta Lane, or Barbican Hill, the church of St. Martin by Looe is soon reached.

Here a Celtic church dedicated to St. Keyne was rebuilt by the Normans, whose impressive north doorway remains, and the old dedication was superseded. The church is mainly fifteenth-century with the usual finely-carved wagon roofs. Modern carved bench-ends and screens have been added.

This was, until 1845, the Parish Church of East Looe, and its long association with the ancient borough is typified by the name heading its list of Rectors: Sir William de Bodrygan, 1280—one of the race who, as its overlords, granted to Looe so many of its early privileges. The south transept was regarded as a "peculiar" of the Looe people and pews were reserved near by for the Mayor and Corporation.

In the aisle, notice the parclose screen erected in 1612 by Langdon of Keverell and ornamented with carved work, including some quaint and naïve mottoes. In the second pier of the arcade is a squint cut to enable the Squire of Keverell to see the preacher. In the south-east corner is an ambitious marble monument, with kneeling effigies, to Walter, the last of the Langdons and his wife (1676).

Seen in the chancel is an interesting incised slate slab displaying the likeness of Philip Maiowe, 1590. Note also, a fine old carved chair; a few Jacobean carved bench-ends in the aisle, and the font constructed from parts of three different fonts, including the original Norman foot.

Regaining the main road, we reach Great Tree caravan camp and, turning to the left by a farm road, pass Longcoe and descend rapidly into the beautiful woods of **Morval.**

Quite close to the Elizabethan *Morval House* we bear to the right, and come at once to the *Church of St. Wenna, Morval.* This, too, is principally fifteenth-century, with Tudor and other additions: the walls have suffered severely from the weight of the wagon roof. On leaving the Church we bear to the left and, crossing the motor road, climb the slopes of **Tregarland Tor.** Following the road around its brow we have entrancing views of the East Looe valley before we descend sharply to the riverside at **Sandplace.**

Ia. To Duloe, Herodsfoot (and St. Keyne)

Distances: From Sandplace Station to Duloe and Herodsfoot, 5½ miles, continuing to St. Keyne and Causeland, 7½ miles.

Rail or road to Sandplace. Then left over the bridge and we climb the hill on a road running through a beautifully wooded glen, now in three-quarters of a mile find on our left hand, bowered beneath a large and leaning bay-tree, **St. Cuby's Well.**

A little Cornish stile mounts the "hedge" and a flagged pavement leads to the arched entrance of a narrow ante-chamber containing a granite bench; whence, through another arch, steps lead down to the water. The well-chamber is crudely vaulted with rubble masonry, and the whole building is on a tiny scale.

"The well at one time was very much respected, and treated with reverence by the neighbouring people, who believed that dire misfortune would befall the person who should attempt to remove it. Tradition says that a ruthless fellow once went with a team of oxen for the purpose of removing the basin.* On reaching the spot one of the oxen fell down dead, which so alarmed the man that he desisted from the attempt. In spite of this tradition, however, the basin has been moved, probably when the new road was cut, and was taken to the bottom of the roads on the Trenant estate." (*Ancient and Holy Wells of Cornwall.*) The basin is now in the church.

At the top of the hill we turn to the right and are soon at the *Church of St. Cuby*, **Duloe.**

This spacious Early-English building is noteworthy for its massive thirteenth-century tower of a type unusual in Cornwall, with buttresses and a pyramidal roof added when the Church was restored in 1860. In the north transept, aisle and chancel is a notable old parclose screen of black oak (fifteenth century). The church also possesses an Elizabethan Communion Cup and cover-paten by John Jons of Exeter, dated 1575. The tomb of Sir John Colshull (1483), shows a full-length effigy of the knight in plate armour and wearing the Lancastrian collar of SS.; but it has been much defaced. Other interesting ancient memorials are in the form of wall slates. The recently restored chapel in the north transept has an altar made from granite taken from beneath the television mast on Caradon Hill. The reredos behind the high altar (by Harry Hems of Exeter) is in Cornish stone including red and gold stone taken from tin mines.

Two hundred yards farther down the main road, on the right, through a builders' yard, is a turning which at once brings into view a small but important **Stone Circle,** of quartz (unique in Cornwall), of which seven stones remain upright and one lies prone.

Returning to the road, we turn right and then take the first turning to the left which brings us soon to the West Looe river at **Churchbridge.** Crossing the stream, we take the second footpath on the right, which leads us through sylvan glades and

* Compare the legend of St. Nun's Well, p. 124.

riverside meadows to **Herodsfoot,** a quaint little village at the conjunction of six valleys, where silver-lead mines were once worked to great advantage. Climbing the hillside by All Saints' Church (built in 1850 when the mines employed over 800 men, and which contains a twelfth-century font), we continue to the top of the hill to the main Dobwalls–Looe road. Here we can either return to Looe by bus or turn left at the main road and take first turning to the right for **St. Keyne's Church.** From the church descend the hill to **St. Keyne's Well** (*see* p. 147) with its interesting legend for newly-weds and continuing along the valley we reach **Causeland** station for the train to Looe.

II. To Talland and Polperro

The usual route from Looe to Talland is by West Looe Hill and the road running past **Portlooe** and close to *Hendersick* farm.

Alternatively: leaving Looe by way of Hannafore, pass the tennis courts and follow the road and through gate at the end. Facing back in the left-hand "hedge" will be noticed a piece of wall some 8 yards long containg two small lancet windows.

This is all that remains of **Monks' House,** the cell provided for an establishment of two monks to minister at the chapel of *Lammana,* which stood on the hillside some two hundred yards distant. It was an ancient foundation, having been in the possession of the Abbot and Convent of Glastonbury as early as 1144. From Monks' House a discarded slipway, much overgrown, leads down to Wallace Beach and remains of an ancient quay.

Follow the cliff edge and cross a tiny stream. Thence a narrow track skirts the western side of Portnadler Bay and the seaward side of **Horestone Head,** but the way often loses itself on the cliff top. It is quite easy though to keep beside the fence until the path becomes clear and leads to **Talland Church.**

The dedication of the church is a matter of some little uncertainty: the "Saint Tallanus" sometimes mentioned seems to have no existence in fact. The older parts of the present structure—the west wall, east window and tower—are attributed to the latter half of the thirteenth century. The rest of the church is fifteenth-century, with a fine example in the aisle of the cradle roofs of that period, ornamented with good carving. Most of the carved bench-ends—in which this church is rich—are of similar age. (Sunday service at 11).

An important feature is the unusually fine carved slate tomb of John Bevyll (died 1578).

From the churchyard there may be seen, on the crown of the western hill, a very ancient manor house (now a farm) called *Killigarth*. This manor, by marriage with the heiress of Beare, passed to Peter Beville, the father of John. John's cousin Matilda was the wife of Sir Richard Grenville of Stowe, and grandmother of that Sir Richard who, in the little *Revenge* surrounded by fifty-three Spanish galleons, "fought such a fight for a day and a night as may never be fought again." This hero's son, Sir Bernard, married in 1592 Elizabeth Beville, a descendant of John Beville here entombed, and became possessed of Killigarth. Their son was Sir Bevil Grenville, the gallant Cavalier leader of the Civil War. This explains the presence of the salient bear of Beare, the bull of Beville and the three sufflues of Grenville, in the armorial shields with which the older woodwork of the church is so freely decorated.

Among other curious tombs, the sepulchral slab of "Jone Mellow and her little sonne" should not be missed.

Talland is one of six Cornish churches which have a tower separate from the main fabric. It is reached from the church by an arcade or long porch, covering a flight of rock steps. In this porch are preserved the old stocks, and there is a good wagon-roof. The terraced churchyard is an unusual feature.

The list of Vicars commences with John Gernays, at the end of the twelfth century; but of all the line none probably is so famous as Richard Doidge, 1713–1746. "Parson Dodge" may, or may not, have had more to do with local "free-trading" than was seemly in one of his cloth. Of his powers as a demon-queller and exorcist there is no doubt, and it is devoutly believed that, catching the Devil one night driving a sable coach and headless horses over the downs of his parish, Doidge, by his "words of power," put His Satanic Majesty to flight forthwith.

Descending the steep hill, and passing the whitewashed cottage at Rotterdam one soon comes out on the beach of **Talland Sand**. The sand is largely in evidence at low water, but the bay is one of great beauty and grandeur. It has been the scene of many wrecks; and although the bathing is good in places, *great care should be exercised* especially in diving from rocks, as there have been several fatalities. The lane leads back steeply from the bay to pass *Talland Bay Hotel*, previously Porthallow House, the principal house in the valley, and parts of which dates back to the sixteenth century.

Walkers will probably be impressed by the gradient of the road leading to Polperro over the summit of the opposite hill. Take comfort, however: from the back of the ruined house by the beach a footpath turns off along the cliff edge which will bring you to your destination without any extraordinary exertion and allow you full enjoyment of the exquisite coastal scenery. Note the War Memorial: a simple, solitary granite cross, high above the sea.

For description of Polperro, *see* pp. 135–8.

Return from Polperro, if desired, by bus. Otherwise return to Talland over the hill-top and take the left-hand turning above the beach. At *Porthallow* farm turn to the right and crossing a stream and climbing another hill by a shady track one comes out at Tencreek Farm near the New Road down to Looe bridge.

III. To Lansallos, Lanteglos and Fowey

From Looe to Polruan by road is 10 miles, four of which may be saved by riding as far as Polperro by bus.

Descend at *Crumplehorn Mill*, and take the road running up the south side of the valley past Langreek Farm. Uphill from the farm is a T junction where turn right. At the following junction bear left for **Lansallos** village.

The church is fifteenth-century, with a Norman font and Norman remains. It is not, perhaps, the finest of this class in Cornwall, but one might certainly describe it as the most typical. Its early history is somewhat uncertain; but there was undoubtedly a church on the site in very early days, and it is suggested that there were rights of sanctuary and asylum. In 1331 the fabric was re-dedicated to St. Ildierna, who may be identical with a certain Bishop Hyldren buried here some time before.

This is a church of no little interest. The carved bench-ends and the wagon-roofs are unusually good; but it is unfortunate that the onslaught of wood-worm has necessitated extensive restoration to the latter. (Sundays 1st and 3rd, 9.30, 4th at 6.30).

From the road by the churchyard wall a lane runs down to the sea at an attractive bathing beach in **Lantivet Bay.** This land is now in the care of the National Trust and the paths are well kept though there is no way for cars.

Those walking straight to Lanteglos (pronounced Lan-*teg*-los) take a footpath from the north side of the churchyard across the fields and the top of West Coombe, saving a detour of 1½ miles by road. The road, rejoined west of Trevarder Farm, is followed for a mile. When Lanteglos Church becomes visible in the valley to one's right, turn down the by-road, which brings one to the churchyard gate in a few minutes.

Lanteglos

The three churches which lie directly between Fowey and Looe (*i.e.*, Lanteglos, Lansallos and Talland) are perhaps the finest examples in the county of the typical minor parish church of Cornwall.

Its exterior is typical: the long, horizontal lines unbroken from end to end; the low-pitched slate roof; the severely plain rubble walls, relieved only by a few well-proportioned windows. Passing into the church by the admirable double-canopy cross, notice how on this side the building is sunk into the hillside. The south-west window, which outside is almost below ground level, from the interior is high above one's head.

A feature uncommon in Cornwall is that three walls of the tower are inside the church. St. Mancus—a hermit—was buried in this church. Notes upon other points of interest will be found on page 106.

Turning R. outside the church, take the first turning on the right and, immediately after, a footpath on the left, which leads into **Polruan** and provides on the way an ever-shifting panorama of Pont Pill, Fowey and the Harbour.

Cross by the ferry from Polruan Quay to Whitehouse, Fowey.

On the return journey, follow the main street of Polruan uphill and across Lantic Downs to gain glimpses of the sea and rocky coastline. From the turning to Lanteglos it is desirable to retrace the outward journey until, between Lansallos and Langreek, one is faced by a fork. Here take the right-hand road, and in a few minutes **Rafiel** (Raphael) is reached.

This ancient manor house (many times rebuilt) is now, in common with many others of like degree, a farmhouse. The manor included at least half, and often more, of the village of Polperro, and when in 1812 the property was sold, one Zephaniah Job of Polperro, often described as "the smugglers' banker", bought the Polperro harbour rights. He discovered, however, that the landed proprietor has responsibilities as well as advantages, for when in 1817 a phenomenal storm demolished the pier, he had to bear the cost of rebuilding, and when, seven years later, the same disaster faced his heir, the latter made haste to dispose of so burdensome an investment.

From Rafiel the road descends rapidly into **Polperro** (*see* pp. 135–8); whence a bus may be used to complete the journey.

IV. To Watergate and Kilminorth

This is a pleasant little round of less than 5 miles. Start from the west end of Looe Bridge up the New Road, and where the boundary-wall of Polvellan leaves the highway, turn rightward into a lane. We pursue the path which accompanies the river more or less closely for 1½ miles to **Watergate,** a few small cottages at the foot of a wooded glen. Turning up the hill here we bear to the left until the farm of *Kilminorth* is reached. An ancient British camp is clearly seen on the hill-top north of the farm.

From this point a field path will lead us back to the right out on to the Polperro road near Wayland.

V. To Seaton Valley and Hessenford

A round of 11 miles. The river *Seaton* rises inland on the moors, and flows to the sea about 3 miles east of, and parallel with, the Looe River. It is worth while taking the coast-road from East Looe, notwithstanding the roughness of the first 2 miles. Do not cross Seaton bridge, at the river mouth, but turn off left and follow the river for nearly 3 miles northward to **Hessenford,** beautifully situated at the intersection of valleys between woods and grassy downs.

Thence, turning sharply to the left and taking the road due west, we follow the bus route to the fork at Shorta Cross and there take the left-hand road, which brings us back to Looe by way of No-man's-land and St. Martin (*see* p. 127).

Alternatively, this walk may be extended from Hessenford up the east bank of the river valley, by way of Roundhouse Bridge. Continue along this road for a short distance, then take the road on the right, to **Menheniot** (rare church with spire), 1¼ miles beyond the railway station. Or continue along the main road and by way of Horningtops reach the railway at St. Keyne.

Polperro

Access.—The nearest railway station is Looe (Western Region), 4½ miles (bus services), but by road Polperro is easily accessible from all parts.

Motorists should see the Motoring section of this Guide.

Accommodation.—*Noughts and Crosses Inn; Claremont; Atlantis Guest House; Landaviddy House; Mill House; Talland Bay.*

Banks.—*Barclays, Midland.*

Bathing is possible towards low tide on a sandy shingle beach outside the pier; but a more satisfactory spot and the general resort, is Chapel (pron. "Chaipel") Pool, among the rocks on the seaward side of Peak. Several sandy coves at the Talland end of the cliff path.

Boating and Fishing.—Pulling boats and motor boats for hire, also trips round coast accompanied by boatmen. Shark fishing with gear and equipment for hire.

Buses.—Regular services to Looe and Plymouth.

Car Parks and garages, some equipped with turntables, border the road leading down. Cars must not—indeed cannot—be parked on the roadway itself for even the briefest period.

Coach Tours.—Day trips to Land's End, St. Ives, The Lizard, Tintagel, Newquay, etc.

Early Closing.—Saturday.

Licensing Hours.—10–2 and 5.30–10.30. Sundays, 12–2 and 7–10.30.

Places of Worship.—*St. John's Church*, 8.30 and 6.30; *Methodist, Wesley*, 11 and 6. *Roman Catholic* (Sclerder Abbey: 1 mile from Polperro on Tallard road).

Post Office.—The Coombes.

Riding.—There are facilities for hiring hacks.

Art Gallery.—The Coombes.

The ancient and charming village of Polperro is undoubtedly the most picturesque in Cornwall.

Imagine a more or less level line of cliffs some 400 feet high, rising almost sheer out of the sea. Imagine, further, some stupendous giant, twenty times greater than Cormelian, arising out of that sea and letting his axe fall slantwise upon the rocky wall so that it is riven from crown to base, and you will have some conception of the situation of Polperro.

In the bottom and upon the lower slopes of a narrow and precipitous winding gorge are huddled the stone-built white-washed cottages of perhaps one thousand inhabitants. They trespass upon one another's walls and foundations to find standing room; they crane their rafters to peep at friends across the way or to glimpse, across their neighbours' ridge-tiles, the triangle of sparkling azure which is the Cornish Sea: they even stand upon one another's eaves to obtain a better view.

And amid all this turmoil, this shoving and shouldering and hoisting and straining of houses, room is found for a river and for several streets, through which cars just manage to squeeze.

The **Harbour,** to which all declivities lead, is a little basin, three acres in extent and dry at low tide, protected by a double quay-head, between which is an entrance so narrow that it is barred against winter storms by horizontal baulks of timber dropped, one after another, into slots in the granite masonry. Outside, the narrow inlet leads obliquely to the open sea, between serrated crags only 50 yards apart.

From the western side of this channel the rocky ground rises sharply to **"Peak",** and thence to the summit of **Hard Head,** at 432 feet. On the seaward slopes of this hill are paths, seats and shelters, which render it a wonderful lounging-place for all. The views are superb.

On "Chaipel" or **Chapel Cliff** (now happily vested in the National Trust) there stood for centuries a chapel which, as *St. Peter de Porthpyre,* is mentioned in an ecclesiastical register of 1392. Twenty-six years later the place-name was written "Porpere"; but when Saxton made his admirable survey in 1576 he wrote it "Poulpery." "Polperro" is therefore most generally supposed to mean either "(St.) Peter's Porth," or "(St.) Peter's Pool."

The village probably came into being as a community of serfs whose duty it was to exploit the fisheries as best they might, and attend to whatever shipping business their lords wished to carry on at this little haven. The manors between which the place was divided were those of Killigarth and Rafiel (*see* p. 133).

The feudal system passed, but the little place has in some ways made little progress. It has never attained to the dignity of urban powers; in secular matter it was divided all through its history, and in ecclesiastical jurisdiction it was no less divided; the stream being the parish boundary between Talland and Lansallos down to 1886, when the whole of Polperro, with St. John's Chapel-of-Ease (built by a Rector of Lansallos in 1838), was declared by Order in Council to be within the Parish of Talland.

For these things the inhabitants, one fears, cared not a rap; their sole desire was to be let alone to go their own sweet way in peace; and in this desire they were remarkably successful. About the opening year of the nineteenth century, however, it was represented to His Gracious Majesty King George the Third that sundry evil-disposed persons in a Cornish hamlet, Polperro to wit, constituted themselves a most outrageous and intolerable nuisance and obstruction to the officers and other loyal and dutiful servants who administered in that part of the dominions His Majesty's laws of Customs and Excise. As a curb upon the activities of these ill-conducted subjects, a boat's crew was stationed in the village, which is said to have been the very first unit in the regular Preventive Service. Polperro folk could make no active resistance to the stationing of these men; but as a matter of course no one would let a room—much less a house—to any of them, and the wretched servants of the Crown were reduced to living aboard an old hulk which they obtained and moored to the quayside. Their presence made little difference, and so long as it continued to pay, smuggling in Polperro flourished. The exploits of its protagonists would fill volumes and cannot be recited here; but many evidences of their activities and ingenuity remain—particularly in the older cottages—in the form of hiding-places, secret entrances and exits, and the like.

The crazy, lime-washed little cottages, many with outside stone staircases, constitute, with the towering wooded hillsides and the rocks, the chief glory of the place; for the charm of Polperro lies less in any individual points of interest than in the general air of rustic simplicity and architectural eccentricity which belong to an age long past. At the side of the old Saxon Bridge, where the stream known as the *Rafiel* joins the head of the inner harbour, is the curious old **House on the Props** (now a restaurant) which, fortunately, is much safer than it appears.

The village is traversed by two main streets, which are interconnected at numerous points by little courts, alleys and lanes. The first comes over Sandy Hill by Killigarth and falls into Polperro with a gradient "like the wall of a house." It seems impossible that a mail coach ever came up (or went down—in safety) such an incline. It accompanies the stream to *Crumplehorn Mill*, perhaps half a mile up the valley, and then

divides: one branch turning sharply to the left and running up a side valley towards Lansallos, the other climbing around the sides of the eastern hill for Pelynt and Looe. The second is one which leaves the Lansallos road at a point some 1½ miles out and descends via the old manor of Raphael into Polperro, at a somewhat break-neck pace, by another fold of the hills; runs through the village parallel to the first and terminates on the Fish Quay by the *Three Pilchards.*

Such, then, is Polperro: a human bees'-nest stowed away in a cranny of the rocks. Its industries are four: the catching of fish, the painting of pictures, handicrafts and—latterly—the entertainment of visitors. Until recently the village was solely a fishing community with a good sprinkling of artists. Of late years, in addition to a large increase in its artistic and literary circle, it has begun to experience some of the less desirable concomitants of fame.

Of unfailing interest to visitors is the **Smuggling Museum** in Talland Street close to the harbour.

For those wishing to make a stay there are comfortable hotels and guest houses, cottage apartments, furnished cottages to let, two small inns and a number of good shops.

The best time to see Polperro is during high water on a sunny morning. In early summer parts of the cliffs are aglow with festoons of the beautiful mauve-pink *Mesembryanthemum*, which, in a good season, flourishes out of doors here as nowhere else in Britain. At several other points amongst the tiers of cottages overlooking the Harbour, its bright and colourful beauty greatly enhances the picturesque grey stone walls.

Eastward by the Cliffs from Looe

1. Seaton, Downderry, Port Wrinkle, Crafthole, and Sheviock. (8½ miles)

Leaving Looe by the cliff path one passes Plaidy Beach, and then Millandreath (*caravan site*), from which after climbing the hill, a walk of about 2¼ miles over the seaside downs brings one to **Seaton.** This is the seaward opening of the Hessenford valley, and it is floored with an extensive stretch of level alluvium, through which the Seaton river winds to a sandy beach. The old cartographers attached considerable importance to this place, which was marked conspicuously on all maps of the sixteenth and seventeenth centuries, under the name of Sothan or Sythye, and possibly even imparted this name to what we now call Whitsand Bay, although the more generally accepted derivation is from White sands. The village is developing as a summer resort, and there are caravan sites and chalets near the road. A hotel (*Eddystone*), some shops, a ballroom and a number of rather attractive residences are scattered about the cliffs.

Adjoining Seaton is **Downderry,** a quite pleasant little place, very popular during the holiday season. Good bathing, sea angling, walks and tennis are among the amenities. There are a few hotels, a number of guest houses, a post office, and the usual shops, a small Church, and a Methodist chapel. Good bus services connect with Looe and Torpoint. Soon after leaving the village, turn through a white gate on the right into a footpath which runs over the hill-top to rejoin the highway by the Armada Beacon. Taking the road over the downs **Port Wrinkle** is soon seen on the shore below, and a steep path, known as Donkey Lane, leads into the village. There is a small harbour with a pier, and there are two well sheltered beaches providing safe bathing at all tides. The old pilchard cellar dating back to the fifteenth century should be visited.

Above the village is a field known as *Round Burrows* where beacons were kept ready to warn of the approach of the Spanish fleet. To the north is a good modern hotel (*The Whitsand Bay*) and a bracing 18-hole Golf Links. On the links to the left hand side of the Port Wrinkle—Crafthole road is an old dove cot erected by the Dawnays in the fourteenth century.

Crafthole is a straggling village on the Downderry—Torpoint road. It was a borough in the reign of Edward II. There are two ancient crosses near by, and a pleasant old Inn (*The Finnygook*).

A typical narrow Cornish road leads to **Sheviock,** a characteristic English wayside village on the A374.

The old church, which was re-dedicated to St. Mary, the Virgin in 1259, may have been founded by St. Fiaac or Feock in the fifth century. The early broach spire is remarkable, the tower is thirteenth century, and the rest of the building probably fourteenth and fifteenth century. The font is possibly Saxon. The wagon-roof of the north aisle, the carved bench-ends and the old stocks should be seen. In the south transept, known locally as the Dawnay Aisle, under a restored canopy may be seen stone effigies of Sir Edward Courtenay and his wife Emmeline Dawnay (1370). Under a window in the north aisle is another effigy of the same period, showing plate armour worn with a bascinet and camail.

Near the church is what remains of the old tithe barn of which Carew wrote: "There runneth a tale how one of the Daunyes ancestours undertook to build the church, and his wife the barne, and on casting up their accounts the barne was found to cost three halfpence more than the churche: and so it might well fall out, for it is a great barne and a little churche." Close to the road towards Antony there is a Holy well, known as Lady well, and from it water is still brought to the church to be used for baptisms.

2. Whitsand Bay, Rame Head, Cawsand, Kingsand and Antony (12½ miles)

For this tour, take the branch road near **Tregantle Fort.** From the summit of the ridge a splendid prospect is spread out, which explains why the Fort was regarded as a most important unit of the Plymouth defences. All the spires, towers and chimneys of The Three Towns lie in full view, with a charming vista of buildings along the water-front; Hamoaze, Lynher and Tamar; Saltash Bridges, the naval anchorage and the Royal Dockyard; all are clearly visible.

Walk around the enclosed area and on reaching the eastern face take, not the first road leading off to the left, but another which runs down towards the cliffs: after rounding the first bluff this turns to the east, and one commences the 4-mile seaside walk to Rame.

This stretch of coast is now a favourite resort of "week-enders" from Plymouth and its environs; their little huts, tents and bungalows dot the hillside at all elevations. A number of masked batteries will also be noticed, all of them obsolete, and *Polhawn Battery*, a massive stone structure of the older type, has even been converted into a private residence.

Visitors succumbing to the temptation to bathe on the pleasant sandy stretches should do so with the greatest caution. East of Port Wrinkle Whitsand Bay becomes a *death-trap to bathers:* a year rarely passes without at least one fatality—and this despite all the warnings so carefully given.

On reaching **Rame** the walker should first visit the curious little church of St. Germanus.

It was reconsecrated in 1259, and contains Norman work; notably one of the few tympana which Cornwall can boast. This is of carved slate, and was discovered in 1885: it is now mounted in the west wall of the aisle. There is a fine old roof with carved ornamentation in the south aisle and some of the old carved bench-ends remain. The hagioscope, rood-loft stairs and seventeenth-century slate slabs should be noticed.

From the church one turns seaward and soon comes out upon—

Rame Head

The conical extremity, which from a distance becomes the most noticeable feature of this promontory, threatens to become entirely insular at some future date: the saddle-back between the peak and the mainland is a well-defined ridge, from which the cliffs descend sharply on either side.

The **Chapel** at the point is perhaps 7 yards long and 3 yards wide inside, with walls upwards of a yard thick. It has a vaulted stone roof and presents an interesting appearance of antiquity. There are four windows and a doorway: the east window is of course the largest, but the framing and tracery are missing from all and the ancient oratory is little better than a ruin. This building is known to have been dedicated in 1397 and 1425 to St. Michael and is thought to have provided (with at least two other chapels) a series of guiding points to the entrance of Sutton Pool, in effect a medieval lighthouse.

On Rame Head too is the site of an ancient cliff castle such as at Tintagel.

At **Penlee Point** no feature is of greater interest than the fog-horn station ("Penlee 'ooter" is the beneficent genie of fog-bound mariners hereabouts). The coastal footpath continues to **Cawsand** and **Kingsand.** These twin towns offer no very striking features save beautiful views alongshore on either hand, and across Plymouth Sound; and the maze of narrow streets, tortuous alleys and irregularly-built cottages so characteristic of Cornish villages. "Cossand" men and boats were foremost in the audacious smuggling exploits associated with the "trade" out of Roscoff in the early part of last century.

Climbing out of Kingsand, one reaches **Maker Heights,** whence again a beautiful panorama of the whole Plymouth district may be enjoyed. Maker Church is the burial-place of the Mount Edgcumbe family, and there is a particularly fine mural tablet to the memory of the fourth Earl, who died in 1917. The tower of this church was used, from the middle of the eighteenth century, as a signal station. Near by, on the north-east of the church, is the ancient holy well of St. Julian.

Mount Edgcumbe Park and the adjacent cliffs now form a country park for public use. **Mount Edgcumbe House** (*open Mon and Tues, May – Sept., fee*), home of the Earl of Mount

Edgcumbe has fine gardens. At the Cremyll end of the park are the popular Orangery Gardens (*free*).

Turning one's back upon **Cremyll** and **Mount Edgcumbe,** and ignoring all side turnings, one is brought by the road, in about 1½ miles, to **Millbrook,** a large village of no special interest which stands at the head of a wide but shallow creek called Millbrook Lake. Bearing to the right along the waterfront and to the left after passing All Saint's Church, one commences the prettiest 2-mile walk to be found in this district. A winding high-banked lane leads through leafy dells, by farmsteads and orchards, to the hamlet of **St. John,** the very model and pattern of what the poets and novelists would have us believe all rustic England to be. Little cottages stand behind tall hedges and luxuriant gardens and farmyards abut upon the road. Beside the stream stands amid elms the squat Norman tower, with pyramidal roof, of a tiny ancient church. The Rectors Plate in the Belfrey commences with John of Exon, 1270. Following the same beautiful road one comes in less than a mile to **Antony.**

This is another quiet, old-world village; but standing as it does on a road which has ever been a main artery for traffic out of Plymouth into Cornwall, it lacks the entire simplicity of St. John. The church is of much interest, and should certainly be inspected. Among the monuments is one to Richard Carew (1555–1620), whose famous *Survey of Cornwall* was published in 1602. **Antony House** (National Trust) is open Bank Holidays, and Tuesday, Wednesday and Thursday afternoons 2–6 p.m. *April–September. Fee.*

From Antony the return to Looe can be made by bus.

St. Germans and Saltash,

though in Cornwall, are too definitely within the sphere of Plymouth to make inclusion in this volume necessary. The grand old church of St. Germans should certainly be seen. It exhibits more Norman work than any other church in Cornwall. St. Germans vied with Bodmin for many years as a religious centre, and until the time of William the Conqueror was the seat of the original Cornish Bishopric, which, after being for years joined to the diocese of Exeter, was revived in

1877, when Truro became the ecclesiastical centre of the county.

The Eddystone Lighthouse

The Eddystone Rocks are situated about 13 miles from Looe, 12 miles from Plymouth Hoe, and 8 miles from Rame Head. They are submerged at high water, lie in the track of ships passing through the Channel and have always been a source of great peril to shipping.

The story of the various attempts to build a lighthouse at this point is a record of disastrous failure and of the ultimate triumph of engineering skill. In 1698, the first lighthouse, a fantastic building, constructed by Winstanley, was completed, only to be almost immediately (1703) washed away in a storm, taking with it by a strange fate its builder, who happened to be visiting Eddystone at the time. All that remained of this work of years was a link of chain in a cleft of the rock.

The second lighthouse was begun in 1706 by Rudyerd, a London merchant. While the work was in progress a French privateer swooped down upon the rock, captured the workmen, and took them off to France, where they were put in prison. Louis XIV heard of the matter. To his honour, he liberated the lighthouse men, and put their captors in their room, declaring that "though he was at war with England, he was not at war with mankind." This building, composed largely of wood, was more successful than the first. There is no knowing how long it would have remained had it not succumbed to fire in 1755.

Two years later, in 1757, John Smeaton turned his attention to the planning of another lighthouse, this time of stone throughout. The material was prepared on land and then conveyed to the rock, where it was all put together in about sixteen weeks, and so securely cemented to the reef that it braved the storms of the English Channel for nearly six score years. The removal of Smeaton's tower was necessary, not on account of defect or wear in the edifice itself, but owing to the disintegration of a portion of the reef. The upper part of the tower was carefully removed and re-erected on the Hoe at Plymouth, where it may still be seen by all.

The fourth and present lighthouse was completed early in 1882, according to the design of Sir James Douglass. There are two lights, the first 133 feet and the second 93 feet above high-water mark. The base of the structure is a solid mass of granite, cylindrical, 20 feet high and 44 feet in diameter, and on this platform the tower is reared. The tower is solid for the first 23 feet; above are nine rooms, each 8¾ feet high. The seven uppermost rooms are 14 feet in diameter, the walls of the lowest rooms being 8½ feet thick. No less than 4,688 tons of stone were used in its construction. The cost of the work was about £60,000. The light, which flashes twice every ten seconds, has a 570,000 candle power. During fog three blasts are given every minute.

The name of the rocks was derived from the fact that there is here no definite tidal current. The ebb and flow of the tide produce only irregular streams and *eddies.*

Liskeard and Neighbourhood

Access.—Liskeard is on the Western Region main line. The journey from London occupies 4 to 5 hours by the fast trains.
Banks.—*Barclays, Lloyds, Midland, National Westminster.*
Buses.—Local services are run by private companies—*see* notices.
Car Parks.—Large car park in West Street; also by Cattle Market; at Sun Girt Lane and Rapson's Field, Station Road.
Distances.—Liskeard is 222 miles from London, 17 miles from Plymouth, 13 miles from Bodmin, and 20 from St. Austell.
Early Closing Day.—Wednesday.
Fishing.—Available on the Looe and Fowey rivers.
Golf.—Bin Down Golf Club, Looe, 18 holes. Tel.: Widegates 247.
Hotels.—*Fountain*, The Parade; *Pencubitt*, Lamellion Hill; *Webb's*, The Parade; *Lux*, Higher Lux Street; *Lord Eliot*, Castle Street.
Hunting.—The East Cornwall Foxhounds and Dartmoor Otter Hounds hunt in the district.
Library.—County Branch Library, Barras Street.
Licensing Hours.—10–2 and 5.30–10.30. Sundays, 12–2 and 7–10.30.
Market Days.—Mondays and Thursdays.
Places of Worship.—*St. Martin's Parish Church*, Church Street; *Methodist*, Greenbank Road, and *Wesley; Roman Catholic*, West Street; *Salvation Army*, Church Street.
Population.—5,360.
Post Office.—The Parade.
Railway.—Liskeard Station (Western Region). Tel.: Liskeard 43319.
Sports.—Sports complex at Lux Park with football, hockey, cricket and tennis. Indoor heated swimming pool. Licensed club rooms. Siblyback Recreational Centre, 4 miles.
Tennis.—Municipal courts in Lux Park.

Liskeard is an ancient market town noteworthy for its cattle fairs, held on the second Monday in each month. The great annual Fair of St. Matthew takes place on October 2.

Though Liskeard is not a holiday resort, many motorists and others passing through are tempted by its attractive appearance to interrupt their journey; and the town is the centre for several interesting short excursions. Five miles to the north is Caradon Hill (1,213 ft.) the site of the formerly prolific South Caradon copper mine and of the far-famed Cheesewring and the Hurlers and now surmounted by a mast of the Independent Television Authority. Near Liskeard also are two well known Cornish Holy Wells—St. Keyne and St. Cleer. The latter stands well up on the Cornish moors. A comparison between these moors and Dartmoor may cause a smile, but there is a good deal of similarity, and the bracing crispness of Caradon air deserves to be as highly esteemed as that of Princetown. Liskeard itself is several hundred feet above sea-level, and is noted for its bracing air. From the Castle Park (475 ft. high) extensive views may be obtained.

The Church (*open daily*) is very fine and the second largest in the county. The granite tower, 85 feet in height, was completed in 1903. There are eight bells, dating from 1735 to 1902. The pulpit—a good piece of carving—bears date 1636. There are "leper" windows at the west end, by the tower and some very fine stained, glass windows. The monuments include one to Joseph Wadham, last descendant of the founder of Wadham College, Oxford. The list of known vicars commences with Martin Pypard, 1263, but there was a church here at a much earlier date. The registers date from 1539. In the south entrance is a quaint notice intimating that pattens must not be worn beyond the porch. Two old Cornish crosses will be seen in the churchyard.

The Reading Room and lending library in the **County Branch Library** are available to visitors. Adjoining the Library is **Stuart House,** where in 1644 Charles I slept for seven nights. There are other ancient and noteworthy buildings in the town.

In Well Lane is the old **Pipe Well,** an interesting and unusual specimen. Four pipes issue from an arched grotto and produce a never-failing supply of water.

Anciently this was called St. Martin's Well, and was much respected. There were only three outlets for the water and that flowing from the middle pipe was supposed to have strongly curative properties, while there was also a superstition regarding the matrimonial prospects of any unmarried woman who touched a certain stone in the cistern with her naked foot.

This source has been more fortunate than many of the Cornish Holy Wells. Although it has been necessary to build over it, the Well remains undisturbed in a carefully kept vault, protected by an iron gate, and retains much of its interest.

The old Liskeard Grammar School (closed 1849) was responsible for the education of several notable men, including John Wolcot (Peter Pindar) and the Rev. R. S. Hawker, the famous vicar of Morwenstow.

Historical Note.—Tonkin derives the name from *Les*, a court or palace, and *Kaer*, a fortified town. The earliest records state that the manor was given by William the Conqueror to Robert, Earl of Mortain, from whom it passed to the Earls of Cornwall. Liskeard was for many years the seat of the ancient princes of Cornwall. Richard, brother of Henry III, granted a charter, dated 1240, to Liskeard, creating it a free borough, and Edmund, Earl of Cornwall (son of Richard), gave the burgesses further privileges, vesting in them nearly all the rights of a corporate town. The corporation in its present form dates from 1586. Leland (1533) wrote: "There was a castle on an hill in the town side, by north from S. Martin. It is now all in ruin, fragments and pieces of walls yet stand. The site of it is magnificent and looketh over all the town. This castle was the Earles of Cornwall's. The walls are now sometimes used as a pound for cattle." *Sic transit Gloria.* The site of the castle is still pointed out, near the church, but probably all the stones have been utilized for other buildings. Liskeard was created one of the coinage towns for Cornwall's tin. During the Civil War, the Royalists made their headquarters here for a short time, and under the command of Sir Ralph Hopton defeated the Parliamentarians in 1643. Liskeard returned two members to Parliament from 1294 until the passing of the Reform Act of 1832, when the representation was reduced to one. In 1885 the town was disfranchised as an independent borough. Among Liskeard's parliamentary representatives may be mentioned Sir Edward Coke (1620), afterwards Lord Chief Justice; and Gibbon (1774), the historian.

EXCURSIONS FROM LISKEARD

St. Keyne Well

Access.—The well is situated on the western hillside of the valley of the East Looe river, 200 feet above the sea and nearly equidistant from two stations, St. Keyne and Causeland, on the Liskeard and Looe branch of the Western Region line. By road the distance is 3½ miles from Liskeard town, with one or two steep hills.

After crossing the main railway line at Liskeard station take the left-hand road at the fork. This falls rapidly into the Looe valley and accompanies the stream and branch railway in a southerly direction; at St. Keyne station a branch road turns sharply to the right, crosses both river and railway by a bridge and bearing again to the left commences to climb the hillside. The well is found about three-quarters of a mile up this slope at its junction with a road running down to Causeland.

"If the husband, of this gifted Well
Shall drink before his wife,
A happy man thenceforth is he,
For he shall be master for life."

St. Keyne was a fifth-century saint. Carew says: "This was not Kayne the man-queller (*i.e.*, man-killer), but one of a gentler spirit and milder sex, to wit, a woman." She was one of St. Brechan's twenty-six children and one of the fifteen who were canonized.

Despite her surpassing loveliness and the rude manners of the age, St. Keyne was able to wander about the country "safe in the strength of her purity," performing astonishing miracles. At Keynsham, in Somerset, for example, she converted a plague of snakes into stone.

After a long and beneficent life the Saint retired to this valley, but not until she was about to die did she endow the waters of her well with their mystic virtue.

Though the St. Keyne Church Council and the Liskeard Old Cornwall Society have endeavoured in the past to maintain the well, the source has now failed, and the water is stagnant.

Southey's quaint poem is well known, but the last few lines demand quotation:

"'You drank of the well, I warrant, betimes?'
He to the countryman said.
But the countryman smiled, as the stranger spoke
And sheepishly shook his head.
'I hastened, as soon as the wedding was done,
And left my wife in the porch;
But i' faith! she had been wiser than me,
For she took a bottle to church!'"

Southey makes Keyne rhyme with seen. The local pronunciation is Kayne.

In returning, the uphill road may be taken to the village of **St. Keyne,** in order to visit St. Keyne's Church, but the building has suffered much "restoration." It is supposed to be of pre-Norman origin and also to be placed upon an early British camp or burial-ground. Three stone heads over the door (reminiscent of St. Piran's church in the sands) seem to be all that support the former supposition so far as material evidence is concerned. The deviation adds less than a mile.

Two miles east of St. Keyne, and on the Liskeard—Plymouth road is **Clicker Tor Quarry,** the largest in east Cornwall. It meets the requirements of the County and District Councils, builders and contractors. It also supplies large quantities of ballast for *British Rail.*

ST. CLEER AND THE CHEESEWRING

The most convenient means of visiting this district from Liskeard is by bus to St. Cleer and Minions.

St. Cleer,

2½ miles due north of Liskeard, has a prominent church tower, 99 feet high, one of the handsomest in the county. It is in three stages. Within the church should be noted the Norman work in the north doorway, the Transition-Norman font, the stocks, and a quaint seventeenth-century slate slab on the tomb of Robert Langeford. A strange feature is that the north arcade is of an entirely different style from the south. There is a fine modern rood-screen.

Not far from the Church, beside the road which passes its east gate, stands the famous **St. Cleer's Well,** with a splendid specimen of a Cornish cross beside it. The baptistery over the well had been allowed to tumble to pieces, but it has been carefully restored with the original stones. The special merit of St. Cleer water was its potency to cure madness.

St. Cleer was, of course, St. Clarus, an Englishman of noble birth who later became a monk. A jealous woman with whom he would have nothing to do had him murdered. Clarus was venerated at St. Clair sur Epte in Normandy.

About a mile beyond St. Cleer Church, in the direction of Caradon Hill, are the **Trethevy Stone,** or cromlech (Trethevy signifies in the Cornu-British language "the place of the graves"). Six large upright stones (a seventh having fallen inward) support a huge table-stone. It is believed that the stones have been in position for at least 2,000 years. Archaeologists have long wondered why the superimposed stone was perforated at one end with a small circular hole. For the benefit of those coming by bus to visit this cromlech it may be noted that the nearest point on the route is *Tremar Coombe,* whence the walk is a short one.

Continuing, the road soon crosses the old rail track and becomes steeper round **Caradon Hill** (1,213 ft.); **I.T.A. transmitter,** wide views of Dartmoor. (For the sake of easier gradients the buses make a detour to the west—note an ancient cross on right-hand side.) This marks the line of the old trackway into Cornwall from Horsebridge over the Tamar. On this same road are the Doniert stones and other crosses. The scenery is wild in the extreme, with huge boulders of granite protruding through the sides of "starved mother-earth." Nearly everything about here is of granite. All round are deserted mines with decayed and falling chimney shafts and buildings. About 2½ miles from Trethevy Stone we reach **Minions Mound,** said to be the burial-place of a king (*Cheesewring Hotel*). Near by are **The Hurlers,** remains of three large Bronze Age circles. The great stones, according to legend, represent players at the famous Cornish game of hurling, who, for playing on Sunday, were turned into stone. A hundred yards to the left of the nearest circle will be noted two stones standing apart—"the two Hurlers who ran after the ball."

Continuing by a moorland track towards the rocky tor which rises out of the heath, after a tough climb over great granite boulders, we reach that wonderful pile of stones, each weighing many tons, called—

The Cheesewring

The balance of the huge stones on the smaller ones beneath is wonderful. The top stone is some 34 feet in circumference and those beneath 17 feet. The pile of stones built up under the large slab as a support in case of need is a modern addition. This great mass of intensely hard, dark, blue-grey granite has maintained its poise from time immemorial. Wilkie Collins described the Cheesewring as "a curiosity that even Science may wonder at: a sight which is worth a visit to Cornwall, even if Cornwall presented nothing else to see."

From the hillcrest above the Cheesewring (1,250 ft.) wonderful prospects over at least half of Cornwall may be enjoyed.

Northward are the waters of the Irish Sea; eastward the bold blue fells of Dartmoor rise into the clouds. To the south one looks out over all the area of this Guide to a sea which shimmers and glints like beaten silver in the sunshine.

With the aid of a glass, Eddystone, with its modern tower beside the stump of Smeaton's masterpiece, appears close in to the shore; a mere chess-pawn to be lifted between thumb and forefinger. Farther to our right an object like part of a match-stick represents the lofty beacon on Gribbin Head and beyond it mile after mile the land runs out to that terror of mariners, the deadly Lizard.

The western horizon is closed by the modest heights of the China Clay country, crowned with silver cones. Close at hand on the north, **Kilmar,** with indented ridges, 1,296 feet high, is a conspicuous object against the skyline. This hill with its tremendous pile of boulders is a grand sight.

At the foot of the last ascent to the Cheesewring is **Daniel Gumb's Cavern,** where a stone cutter endowed with a remarkable mathematical mind lived with his family in the eighteenth century. Cut on a slab of granite which formed the roof of his strange dwelling is a figure intended to prove Euclid's forty-seventh proposition, and on a smaller stone at the side is the inscription by his own hand: "D. GUMB 1735."

The original "cavern" collapsed owing to quarrying; the inscribed stones, however, are the actual ones wrought by Gumb. See Hawker's *Footprints of Former Men in Cornwall.*

Before leaving the Caradon district yet another interesting monument of antiquity may be seen. About a mile north-west of St. Cleer, close to the road from Darite to Redgate, are two stones. One is about 7 feet 6 inches high, 2 feet 6 inches wide, and a foot thick, roughly ornamented with a panel of interlace. This is a cross shaft and on the top is part of a mortice, evidently cut for the reception of another stone. The adjoining stone, called the **King Doniert Stone,** has the inscription: "DONIERT ROGAVIT PRO ANIMA," a monument to Doniert, one of the early kings of Cornwall, said to have been drowned about 872. (Visitors should note that these curiosities are best known to the countrypeople as "The King's Stones.")

Between St. Cleer and St. Neot, in the lovely valley of the Fowey river, about 4 miles from Liskeard, may be seen the picturesque **Golitha Falls.** These Falls are best reached from Dreynes Bridge by a half-mile walk through woods beside the river.

ST. IVE AND CALLINGTON

Distances from Liskeard.—St. Ive, 4¼ miles; Callington, 8½ miles.
Buses connect with Saltash, Tavistock, Liskeard, etc.

St. Ive

St. Ive (pronounced St. Eve) has a fine church of the Decorated period, dedicated to St. Ivo. Granite predominates in all parts of the structure. Note the unusually fine old wagon-roofs, the hagioscope and sedilia; the brightly-tinctured Royal Arms of Charles II, dated 1660 and of heroic proportions, the parish stocks, and the sundial over the south porch inscribed "Quotidie morior 1695." Best of all is the fine east window with its beautifully wrought stained glass and graceful niches on its sides. The very fine tower, with its quartet of triple pinnacles, should also be noticed.

The Church of **Quethiock** (pronounced "Quethick" and believed to have connection with St. Cadoc) two miles south of St. Ive, is worth the journey. It now bears the rare dedication to St. Hugh of Lincoln and boasts a tower very unusual in these parts, apparently rising chimney-wise out of a roof end instead of seeming to stand on a separate base. In the churchyard is an ancient carved cross reputed the second highest in Cornwall but the shaft is not a monolith. The Church has fine wagon-roofs, rood-loft stairs and hagioscope, and the stocks are to be seen in the porch. In the floor is a brass bearing date 1471 to Roger Kyngdon, Joanna his wife and sixteen children all depicted in costume. On a wall is another to Richard Chiverton (died 1617) and Isabel his wife (whose grandson, Richard, was a Sheriff of London, 1650–51; in 1657 he was the first Cornishman to become Lord Mayor of London and was knighted by Cromwell in 1658).

There is a slate memorial of Hugh Vashmonde, 1607, and a more imposing one to Obadiah Ghossip, Rector of St. Tudy in the Cromwellian period. The nine stained-glass windows, one of St. Cadoc, were actually designed and made in Quethiock by the Rev. W. Willimott, Vicar, circa 1870 (a fragment of medieval glass is incorporated in one north window). The high altar, low screen and other details are in carved oak by the same hand.

The organ is the result of the industry of a subsequent vicar (J. A. Wix) who made and sold whips and walking sticks to raise the money.

At **Newbridge,** between St. Ive and Callington, the road crosses the Lynher river by an angularly-recessed bridge, set in a scene of great rustic beauty. South-west of the bridge looms the almost conical height of Cadson Bury, its brow encircled by a tremendous earthwork.

Callington

Access.— (*a*) By bus from Liskeard. Saltash, Launceston, Tavistock, etc. There is a bus service with Plymouth via the new Tamar Bridge.
(*b*) By rail to Saltash, thence by bus.
Banks.—*Barclays, Lloyds, National Westminster.*
Car Park.—Next to Bus Station.
Distances.—Calstock, 5½ miles; Liskeard, 8½; Tavistock, 10; Saltash, 9.
Early Closing Day.—Thursday.
Hotels.—*Bull's Head.*
Post Office.—Fore Street.

Callington, now a small, though not unattractive, town, was once a parliamentary borough returning two members. It seems never to have had a corporation, being governed by a Portreeve and Reeve elected, with other officials, at the Court Leet of the manor of Kelly-Land. Of the insignia there remain the Portreeve's chain and a silver mace. The town is within the area of the Caradon District Council.

It is an article of popular belief that King Arthur kept his court here in the sixth century, the place being then called Killiwick. In Domesday Book it is registered as one of the King's towns, under the name of Calweton. In 1267 it received a market charter from Henry III.

The **Parish Church of St. Mary**, an imposing granite edifice, was rebuilt in 1438 by Nicholas Assheton, one of the King's Judges, who, habited in the judicial costume of the period, is portrayed with his wife in a brass on the chancel floor.

This is one of the few Cornish churches that have anything in the nature of a clerestory: there are three little windows on the south side of the nave and four on the north. The roof and double arcade seem to indicate that the north aisle was added to the church in a somewhat unusual fashion.

On the north side of the chancel is the alabaster tomb, with life-size effigy of the first Lord Willoughby de Broke (died 1502), who was Steward of the Duchy of Cornwall, Lord of Kelly-Land, and patron of this living. His armour is a fine suit of plate, the mail hauberk showing at neck and thigh. At his left knee is the Garter, and he wears also the Mantle, Collar and George of that most noble Order. At his feet are two small figures of friars. Although shamefully defaced, this fine monument is of great interest.

There is a Norman font, with numerous fragmentary remains of other antiquities.

In the churchyard should be noticed the ancient double-canopied cross of granite, much the worse for wear.

Len Harvey, the famous boxer, one-time champion of England, was born near Callington.

Dupath Well

Access.—Leave the town by Tavistock Road and at the "four-went-ways" half a mile out take the road indicated by the guide-post as leading to Dupath Well Chapel. The first left-hand turning out of this runs down to the gate of a farmyard. Enter here and pass down the side of the farm buildings. In a few moments the small chapel appears on the right hand.

Architecturally this is the most important of all Cornish Holy Wells, for whereas in most cases there is little more than a tiny arch or vault over a cistern sunk in some bank or hillside, here we have a distinct chapel, or baptistery, of some size, with doorway and window-mullion of dressed stone.

The walls are of roughly-squared granite blocks, and the roof of granite bars, supported at their outer ends by the walls and in the middle by a rude arch. On the west wall above the door is the finial which forms so remarkable a feature of the building: two upright slabs support on their bevelled upper edges a sculptured pinnacle suggestive of some outlandish crown.

The water enters beneath the threshold, flows across the paved floor in a gutter to a rectangular trough, or "well," extending almost from wall to wall, and through a hole beneath the east window into a cylindrical basin outside, whence it finally escapes.

Some of the blocks of granite used in the structure are of notable size; there is one in the east wall more than 11 feet long, extending the whole width of the building.

The legend connected with the building of the Well is to the effect that two Saxons, Sir Colan, an impoverished knight, and Gottlieb a wealthy commoner, fought here for the hand of a lady whom both admired. The remainder of the story is obscured by contradictions between different versions; but the survivor is generally credited with having built the baptistery and living "happily ever after". The Well Chapel is now in the care of the Department of the Environment.

Kit Hill

This is the eminence a mile and a half from Callington which stands out so prominently for miles around, being the only elevation of note between the Caradon moors and the Tamar. Rising to 1,091 feet and crowned with a tall and somewhat ornate mine chimney resembling a beacon tower, Kit Hill is a conspicuous object to all travellers between Plymouth or Tavistock and Looe or Liskeard, and the summit may be reached by road.

It is the western termination and most elevated part of **Hingston Down,** that Hengist's Down whereon the enterprising Teutons Hengist and Horsa encamped after fighting their way into Cornwall in the mid-fifth century; the hill, moreover, whereon in 836 Egbert, in fact if not in name first King of the English, routed a combined army of Norsemen and Cornish Britons. Arrowheads and other relics are discovered from time to time and there were important earthworks. The latter, however, have been much damaged in more recent times by mining operations, whereby the hillside now shows a succession of excavations and "dumps."

"Hingston Down well wrought
Is worth London dear bought"

ran the old rhyme; but this seems no longer credited for the mine buildings are in ruins and the mineral treasures lie undisturbed.

ST. NEOT

Access.—By car, 6½ miles from Liskeard, 9 miles from Bodmin. There are few if any buses. For walkers from Liskeard it is a gruelling walk across the hills.

Such was the fame of St. Neot that wonderful stories are still told of him. When he discovered that his parishioners could not come to church, because their presence was needed to scare away crows from the crops, he caused the crows to be impounded every Sunday! The Crow Pound still exists on Goonzion Downs. St. Neot has been claimed as a relative of King Alfred, and the book of Hyde, 1200 says: "Alfred went to Cornwall and repaired to the Church of St. Gueryr, where St. Neot reposes for the alleviating of his illness." It has even been said that St. Neot was Alfred's elder brother, who resigned the crown to his junior in order to lead the life of a hermit.

The Church of St. Neot has a magnificent series of late fifteenth- and early sixteenth-century stained-glass windows, famous throughout the West of England. They are quite beyond any possibility of rivalry in Cornwall—a county not rich in this class of ecclesiastical ornament—and as an aggregation of early glass can have few equals elsewhere. Some of the features are unique. In 1937–9 the windows which had been restored in 1825 by J. P. Hedgeland were carefully repaired. The subjects are as follows (beginning at the East chapel window and travelling round the church clockwise):

(1) The *Creation window*. This is considered to be a good specimen of fifteenth-century work. The design represents the Deity planning the world with a pair of compasses, followed by fourteen events up to the time of Noah.

(2) The *Noah window* shows a continuation of the same object (15th cent.)

(3) The *Borlase window*. (4) The *Martyn window*.

(5) The *Mutton window*. (6) The *Callawy window*.

(7) The *Tubbe and Callawy window*.

(8) *Armorial window* (Hedgeland).

(9) *St. George window* (15th cent.).

(10) The *St. Neot's window* records in twelve designs the legendary history of the Saint:

(*a*) St. Neot resigns his crown to Alfred the Great, who kneels to receive it.

(*b*) The Saint takes the vows of a monk. The abbot reads the vows, whilst a monk covers his head with a cowl.

(*c*) St. Neot reads the Psalter, with his feet immersed in his favourite well. Rescues a doe from a hunter, who, struck with awe at the miracle which has preserved the doe from the dogs, delivers his horn to the Saint and afterwards turns monk himself.

(*d*) St. Neot receives instructions from an angel respecting three fishes which he shows him in his well. These instructions were that so long as he took one, and only one, for his daily food, the supply should never diminish.

(*e*) The Saint, ill in bed, desires his servant Barius to bring one of the fish for dinner as usual.

(*f*) Barius, anxious to suit his sick master's appetite, takes *two* fishes from the well, of which he boils one, and broils the other on a gridiron.

(*g*) Barius brings the two fishes on a dish to his master in bed.

(*h*) Barius sent back by the Saint in alarm at his having transgressed the angel's instructions. He throws the fish again into the well, when they are restored to life.

(*i*) A thief drives away the Saint's oxen from before the monastery.

(*j*) A man and boy ploughing with four stags, which at the Saint's prayers came and offered themselves tamely to the yoke in lieu of the stolen oxen.

(*k*) One of the robbers, terrified at this miracle, brings back the oxen to the Saint, in consequence of whose instruction he and his companions become monks and enter the monastery.

(*l*) St. Neot kneels to receive Pope Martin's blessing.

(11) The *Young Women's window* represents St. Patrick, St. Clere, St. Mancus and St. Brechan(?). Beneath these are twenty female figures representing the donors of the window.

(12) The *Wives' window*, with St. Mabena, the Virgin Mary, the Saviour, and St. Mewbred or Mebered. Beneath are twenty female figures representing the donors.

(13) The *Harys window*. (14) *Redemption window* (Hedgeland).

(15) *Acts window* (Hedgeland).

(16) The *chancel window* is an early nineteenth-century (Hedgeland) copy from the earliest representation of the Last Supper that could be found in the British Museum.

Note the fine barrel-roofed porch with upper chamber, the font and the massive tower, and the richly carved pinnacles of tower, porch and roof.

On the north side of the chancel is the desecrated tomb of the Saint. For a time his remains lay in peace within the sarcophagus; but the wave of relic-worship reached even to this secluded hamlet, and the venerated skeleton was removed entire (save for one arm) to the Benedictine Monastery in Huntingdonshire which afterwards gave the name of St. Neots to a neighbouring town.

The churchyard has five ancient crosses, including the decapitated one which is regarded as "St. Neot's," and has a well-ornamented shaft. The head of a cross recently discovered in the churchyard is thought to be the missing one.

St. Neot's Well, less than half a mile from the Church, was restored in 1852. (Take turning on right of *Carlyon Garage*.)

A mile along the road to Two Waters Fort (A38) are the **Caverns of Carnglaze**, old underground slate quarries now opened to the public.

Index

INDEX